Rea

Female Leadership

Introduction

In the summer of 2020, Pema Nooten sent me a message 'can we meet?'. In that request was a given: we wouldn't be meeting in person. It was just a few months into the COVID-19 pandemic. Something none of us will forget. As I write this, it's still in our lives, 20 months later. We had the conversation and in it, she expressed the fact she missed the connection with the members of the network we both belong to, the Professional Women's Network (PWN) NL. Pema had recently joined, just a few months prior to the pandemic. Now, we were no longer meeting in person. All contact had gone online. Not unfamiliar now but back then we were still adjusting (may I say reeling) from the effects of this imposed quarantine.

Both of us had a couple of common interests: creating workspaces / places in which people can thrive, as well as improving global female leadership. Pema had recently published a collaborative book with 17 other authors. From this, we reached the idea to invite PWN NL members to contribute to a book of essays.

Though this book is not sponsored by PWN NL, the network has supported its creation. The essay topics cover the pillars of PWN NL:

- Emotional Intelligence
- Career Development
- Data/Tech Intelligence
- Financial Intelligence
- Men as Allies
- Mentoring
- Networking

All are needed to support women in advancing in their careers and to be leaders in their field.

We take great pride and pleasure in presenting this book to you, the reader: a collection of essays by a group of 28 women and men who want to contribute to creating gender equality NOW! We hope, with sharing our thoughts and research on these topics, together with our individual calls to action, you will join us in making a difference.

We are also proud and grateful that all authors were willing to forgo receiving any proceeds and all profits after costs of the book sales will be donated to a charity supporting (young) women in developing their leadership skills. For more information please visit our website www.readyforfemaleleadership.com

Mary Jane Roy and Pema Nooten
Co-Founders and Co-Authors
Ready for Female Leadership: The Future is NOW

1 Marlene de Koning

Marlene de Koning *joined Microsoft in 2019 to enhance and scale a new Microsoft Solution called Workplace Analytics. This solution transformed into one of Microsoft's new businesses called Viva.*

In 2012, she joined LinkedIn as one of their first solutions consultants to bring new LinkedIn solutions to the market. She was responsible for the adoption and growth of digital Media and New Products into the Enterprise businesses and to bring digital transformation to her clients. Before joining LinkedIn, she worked at both IBM and for brand/research agencies.

She is a public speaker at events such as: Women in Tech, CHRO Forum EMEA, Talent Connect London/Las Vegas, HR Vision Event, and the World Employer Brand Event. Her main focus is on how business can solve their problems and scale through innovative technologies.

One of her passions is driving gender balanced leadership change for the next generation. It's one of the reasons she dedicates her time and talent as a volunteer and mentor.

→ *To contact Marlene: Linkedin.com/in/marlenedekoning*

An Equal Society Starts with Resiliency and Using Your Voice

I was born and raised in the Netherlands and have spent most of my adult life in this country, except for a few years when I lived abroad and during all my travels. Due to my international jobs and personal interest in travel, I have experienced different (work) cultures and learned about all the greatness this country has to offer. But I am also confronted every day with how we are lagging behind in this country, and just how misogynistic some parts of our culture are.

I have the support of many special people in creating my professional success. The help of my mom, who takes care of my children; my husband, who supports me in many decisions; and 'the village' helping me raise my children. Without them, I wouldn't be where I am today. They are my sounding boards in career and life decisions. I realize I'm privileged to be surrounded by so many who cheer me on. However, I'm also confronted with the opinions of some who say I'm selfish to choose (financial) independence and work over home.

My parents have invested in my education, as did the social system of this country. I want to use my time and talent to give back to our society. I genuinely believe we need to do it together and uplift each other. In this way, we will reach our maximum professional potential and will benefit as a social society. This isn't a road I can take on my own. It is the reason why I became part of the PWN network and started to share my time and talent to the network. For me, true leadership is not about making myself better but making everyone around me better, so we grow collectively. There is still so much room to grow to reach gender balanced leadership, especially in the Netherlands. But it's not something one person can reach on their own; we all need to chip in to get there as a community and society.

Enable and uplift each other

Here is an example of the network at work: two members of the network encouraged me to get involved in the Azure academy, where I studied data science. This pivoted my career and landed me my role as a director within a product engineering group at Microsoft. "Growth and comfort do not co-exist", is what Ginni Rometty said years ago, and has been something of which I have been a firm believer. From hospitality to data science is a road of discomfort. Launching new products and being on the early adopter side of the curve, saw me fighting battles and standing up for what I believe in. And I am applying the same to reach more equality.

The discomfort has reached an ultimate high for me the past year. Since 2020, every member of society, including myself, is facing existential questions as result of the pandemic. As a parent, I struggle with what practices I should adopt to alleviate the stress on myself and my family. This, while trying to maintain business KPIs, customer commitments and relationships.

If we want to see a change or at least make the best out of this or any situation, I honestly believe we need to enable and uplift each other. In this way, everyone can maximize and reach their professional potential. We cannot do this on our own. With our allies we will be able to reach our goals better and faster.

The strategy I set when I became president of PWN NL in 2019, is to invest in emotional intelligence, financial intelligence, as well as tech and data intelligence.

For me, these three pillars are connected, and each is important for different reasons. Firstly, during the lockdown, I realized that Tech and Data intelligence is knowing which tools to use to stay connected. It's also about how to make use of the digital world to prevent isolation. It's equally important for the people who shifted to remote work and have been impacted by being 'always on'. In my role at Microsoft, my team works on a solution that helps people understand how they work. This also helps them to understand how they can be better connected, to have the time to focus on the right tasks at hand, and to reduce the overload of meetings. But still, with the move to remote working, we see that 7 out of 10 employees have increased their after-hours work[1]; more than 50% of people feel overwhelmed and stressed[2]; and women are taking a heavier 'chore load' during this pandemic[3].

Secondly, Emotional Intelligence is often referred to as the power skills you need to thrive as a leader in the corporate world or as an entrepreneur. But in my view, reducing stress in our lives, learning to prioritize, and saying no both at work and in our personal lives, also takes a lot of emotional intelligence.

Finally, there is Financial Intelligence. Much research shows women could grow and have their personal and financial affairs in better order. They need to think about investments and pension planning. Also, in business, financial intelligence is a key skill required to be able to lead. As an entrepreneur, it is essential to do your own P&L (Profit & Loss) statements and financial planning. As a senior manager or leader in a corporate, you need to know how to request and negotiate with FP&A (Financial Planning & Acquisition). What deeply concerns me, is that 50% of women are not financially independent[4] and women still earn less than men. They also lose a significant amount of pension by taking career breaks to have children.

We are focused on maximizing the professional potential of women and work with our partners for gender balanced leadership. However, research shows it's vital that personal and family wellbeing needs are taken care of, to thrive at work. To engage your personal partner, split the caregiving tasks which take up so much of our time.

My hope for the future is that the next generation will work and live in a more equal society. That the leaders of tomorrow will show different and more inclusive behaviors than the leaders of today. By investing part of our time and talents in addressing community, societal, country, or global issues, we can drive change for the next generation. I want to do my part and I'm always open to learn more on how I can contribute.

Take a page out of my playbook

I implore you to take some of the steps I have taken. I am a mentor and sometimes coach of other women, both internally and externally. I speak at summits and symposiums. I recommend women for sponsorship within their organization. A sponsor is someone senior (2-3 levels above you) within the company, with whom you have a relationship, who values your skills. They basically advocate for you when you're not there. They have access to people you don't have access to. They tap people on the shoulder for positions they hear are opening up. If you want to be on the list of such positions opening up, you need someone to recommend you. You are top of mind for that person. And you've both agreed on this this; you know they're talking about you. They may also give you projects so you can demonstrate different skills in an area you're currently not in. Make it 'formal', so the sponsor knows what you want to do, where you want to go. Otherwise, there may be too little obligation on their part. 'A coach talks to you, a mentor talks with you, and a sponsor talks about you.'

Find out what you really want for yourself and ask for it, since people are not mind readers. If you don't share what you need, what you want, or where you want to get to, it's unlikely you will get there.

Keep your hard and soft skills up to date. No matter what position you are in, you need to grow with the new technology. You need to know what you are asking for, and what you are investing in to get your budget in line. Rotate your hard skills and soft skills trainings. Every quarter or six months, take a course in either one of these.

Understand that not all decisions are made in meeting rooms. Build relationships with the right people. Think ahead and get those people in your corner. Make sure you have someone who will either articulate your voice or get you into the meeting.

Single out and create a bond in the beginning with some people and work with them, so they can accelerate your voice. Later, they will help you to 'own the right' to let your voice be heard. If you cannot get the leader in the group (not necessarily the person highest in rank) on your side, then it is a very hard battle to fight.

Own the room! Understand that if you are there, you belong there. Always tell yourself that your voice matters. If you are there, then you want your voice to be heard. Otherwise, why are you there? If you are only there to listen, you can listen to a recording or read the notes.

There is a difference in being right and getting the right to say something and having people acknowledging you. The latter is something you might need to work on. There can be many reasons why people don't give you that right. If you build relationships one on one within the group, it's easier to get the group's permission. Find out the commonalities between yourself and the others, to bridge any gap.

A Call To Action!

Things need to be done. Who is going to do it? Raise your hand, admit you do not know how to do it but you know you can learn it. That is how to gain a lot of skills and if we all do that, I believe we grow as a community and as a society to create a better future for the next generation.

Know what your gap is. Ask people around you what they feel you lack. Ask what you might not be aware of. This could be skills, experience, branding etc.

Remember: you can achieve a lot on your own but way more with others around you.

Footnotes

1 https://workplaceinsights.microsoft.com/workplace-analytics/balancing-work-and-life-under-one-roof/

2 https://www.qualtrics.com/blog/confronting-mental-health/

3 https://data.unwomen.org/publications/whose-time-care-unpaid-care-and-domestic-work-during-covid-19

4 https://digitaal.scp.nl/emancipatiemonitor2020/hoeveel-vrouwen-zijn-economisch-zelfstandig/

2

Dick Rüger

***Dick Rüger** is the founder of DARe2Change. He believes in people's ability to transform and grow. That's why he helps clients to discover their (inner) needs, passion, and purpose, while acknowledging their challenges and conflicts. Dick coaches individuals, relationships, teams, and organizations. His purpose in life is to help others thrive by 'offering you his hand, so you can cross those wild rivers.' Dick spent 25+ years in the cross cultural international corporate world in (senior) management and project lead positions. He has crafted businesses from scratch and helped to implement strategy at operational and corporate level.*

Dick lives in Bloemendaal, close to the beach and the dunes. He considers himself very fortunate to be able to use this inspiring nature as his office and coaching practice. He is married with two adult children. He's an active member of the Rotary Club Amsterdam West. Dick loves long-distance running and combines that with yoga, classical music, and food.

→ *To contact Dick: linkedin.com/in/dickaruger*
dare2change.eu

We Need to Use EI & Other Qualities (More)

After the Industrial Revolution and the Second World War, the Service Economy developed in the '50s of the previous century. The work of craftsmen and masters changed and this, amongst other reasons, led to the creation of the 'white collar' manager. This manager was a man (at that time, it was almost always a man), who determined the strategy and organized the tasks and people. He told you what you had to do, when you had to do it, and often even how you had to do it. His role and position were based on his experience and knowledge. He who knew the most was frequently seen as the most valuable player and hence picked for the position of CEO.

However, with the arrival of the internet, and more specifically the world wide web, this changed dramatically. Suddenly, knowledge was widely available with the click of a mouse. Hence the role of the manager changed. He or she had to focus much more on motivating and developing people. The directive manager was being replaced by the inspiring leader. This also created opportunities for women, as access to knowledge was no longer a blocking factor. More importantly, women in general are quite good in motivating and developing others.

Not sure whether it was the spirit of the times or just coincidence, but around the same time that the world wide web started, the concept of Emotional Intelligence (EI) was launched. In 1995, Daniel Goleman published 'Emotional Intelligence'. In this book, he defined Emotional Intelligence as "the capacity for recognizing our own feelings and those of others, for motivating ourselves and for managing emotion well in ourselves and in our relationships."

Daniel Goleman recognized 4 dimensions of Emotional Intelligence:

- Self-awareness or knowing your inner state
- Self-management or controlling and improving your own behavior
- Social awareness or tuning into other people (empathy)
- Relationship management or dedicating time and energy into your relationships

From recent research, we know that the higher one is on the corporate ladder, emotional intelligence becomes increasingly more important. Effective leaders must master all four dimensions. Moreover, it turns out that except for self-awareness, women score on average better on three of these four dimensions than men!

In a Forbes article on October 9th, 2019, Dr. Shawn Andrews states that "men and women have been shown to be equally emotionally intelligent," but that "men and women possess different EQ strengths or competencies that are considered gender-specific." She links this with differences in the upbringing of boys versus girls. As a result, "men outperform women in the EQ skills of assertiveness and confidence, and women outperform men in the EQ skills of empathy and interpersonal relationships."

Considering the earlier described shifting need from manager to leader, one would have expected that organizations have become less patriarchal and more matriarchal. At the very least, we could expect them to be more blended. Although I see this shift is happening, it is still fairly limited. Last year (2020), only 37 of the Fortune 500 CEOs were women and the trend in Europe isn't much better.

So where do things go wrong?

We know that there are various elements hampering the faster rise of female power. These include the glass ceiling, motherhood as a 'dent' in your career and the fact that it may take a generation or even two, to create a sustainable mindset change benefiting women. Still today, people tend to hire people who look like themselves. This happens consciously but even more so, unconsciously. So, as long as men are ultimately responsible for hiring or for writing the algorithms used for this, women will still be at a disadvantage. It will take quite some additional time to really see a change, I'm afraid.

There is something though, that might help women to climb the ladder faster and higher, if they want to, of course. And that is Emotional Intelligence.

In today's volatile, uncertain, chaotic, Covid and ambiguous (VUCCA) world, effective cooperation is crucial. In recent years, we have discovered that next to resilience and adaptability, it is also crucial that you understand yourself and others well. As a leader, you can then use this knowledge to lead yourself and your people better, in an environment where change is the only constant.

Why don't women use their superiority in emotional intelligence?

In all fairness, I don't really know the answer to this question, as I haven't found any serious research on this topic yet. From my own experience as an executive coach and as a person interested in female behavior, I do have some ideas though. This comes with a cautionary note: please be aware that as a man, I am most likely biased.

First of all, self-awareness and the self-efficacy of women can be limiting. Whereas men consider themselves (more than) qualified if they think they master 60% of the required skills and competencies, women start to feel somewhat comfortable by 80% or even 90%. And even then, women tend to focus more than men on the gaps they have. This can become a hurdle for women to take that caring step, to go after that great promotion or that new better paid or rated job.

Secondly, aspects of Emotional Intelligence like empathy are often considered as 'soft'. Showing your Emotional Intelligence may conflict with the old school profile of an assertive, independent, and decisive manager. At the end of 2020, I heard an interview with a power woman who was facilitating many high level, heavy negotiations with very tough people. She mentioned it helped in her work that she by nature shows a lot of empathy. She also stated she sometimes struggles with this soft, female aspect which seems to come naturally to her.

Elements like empathy, compassion, and building good personal relationships are often seen as female qualities but not as key competencies for leaders. And, although I see a clear shift in the public debate, I still come across (too) many men, in too many organizations, for whom these elements are soft and maybe even scary or threatening.

The fact these competencies are more difficult to measure and hence difficult to reward, is also not helpful. It's much easier to assess someone on hard performance KPIs, like turnover, profit, growth and employee retention than to look at underlying emotional aspects of leadership. However, I am a strong believer that Emotional Intelligence will help an organization to prosper operationally, financially, and more importantly, as a human organism.

Thirdly, Emotional Intelligence can also be limiting your effectiveness as leader. Sometimes you have to take difficult decisions, like a reorganization or a 'negative' assessment, which impact individuals, teams or whole departments. Too much empathy and compassion, can then make it feel difficult for you to make these decisions in a non-judgmental, objective way. However, you should not hesitate on such decisions because of your empathy, compassion or simply your relationship with someone. People sense when something negative is coming their way. Leaving them 'hanging' is highly unfair and stressful for the person. Or in the words of Brené Brown: "Clear is kind. Unclear is unkind."

Be aware that after you have taken the tough decision, Emotional Intelligence becomes highly important when going into the execution phase. You must approach this process with even more empathy and compassion. You need to dedicate more time, attention, and energy to the relationship with both the people impacted and those who are not. Attention for the latter group is as important. They will notice and judge you on how 'humanely' you convey the message to the people impacted.

Fourthly, using your Emotional Intelligence on purpose may sometimes be viewed as manipulative. As long as it's done with the best intentions it may be manipulative, but not in the negative sense of the word. Hence no reason not to use your emotional intelligence, as long as it's done with integrity.

Lastly, using your emotional intelligence can be quite scary. It may require you to show and share your vulnerability in an environment or situation where you don't know how people will react. This requires courage.

But there's also good news!

As mentioned before, the role and characteristics of a manager have changed. To ensure a productive, robust, and agile organization in today's VUCCA world, managers have to transform into agile leaders. These are leaders who, in the first place, are able to create psychological safety in relationships: who empower people, who are active (empathetic) listeners and also reflective, who are willing to change their mind/viewpoint, and who use their emotional intelligence skillfully. Or, in the words of maestro Bernard Haitink: Leaders who "embrace the orchestra without suffocating them."

From my years as a manager, leader, and coach in large, international profit organizations, I have come to the conclusion that women, like men, in general have the qualities to be good agile leaders and to some extent maybe even more so than men.

A Call to Action!

Therefore, I call on and urge you, women and men as well, to focus more on your female qualities as described above, including emotional intelligence and agile leadership qualities. Apply them for your own benefit, as well as for the benefit of your employees, the organizations you are working for or are involved with and for society as a whole. This is even more important, as the younger generation is demanding this. Without Emotionally Intelligent, agile leaders they will turn their back on the organization and search for places where they do find these qualities in their leaders (and purpose, of course).

I also have a last note of warning; don't forget to apply the other, male qualities as well. These are as important to create and lead a sustainable, 'human' organization as are the female traits.

Don't be shy: use all the marvelous masculine and feminine qualities you already have in you.

Disclaimer: this article is based on my own private ideas and convictions. It may contain generic statements some people may not agree with.

3

Vivian Acquah

Vivian Acquah *is an inclusive Workplace Wellness Advocate. She advises managers on how to keep their team members engaged, energized, and safe in a sustainable manner.*

Vivian is making topics related to workplace wellness & DEI accessible to everyone. She provides people with the right tools, at the right time, to embrace inclusive changes. She motivates people to think consciously and inspires them to take action.

In 2020, Vivian's son Orlando inspired her to create a movement where every year more than 60 professionals around the world are changing the narrative by creating a ripple effect to amplify diversity, equity, and inclusion. This movement is called Amplify DEI.

Vivian's mission is to help make the world a better place by creating thriving workplaces for EVERYONE. This is a promise not only to Orlando and his generation but also for future generations.

→ *To contact Vivian: linkedin.com/in/vivianacquah*
amplifydei.com | vivalavive.com

Amplifying Your Career Through Mentorship

A mentor is someone who shares their experience and expertise with you, helping you to set priorities, overcome challenges, and make good career choices. When I started my career, I was not aware of the significant benefits of having a mentor; someone supporting me in pursuing opportunities, providing reliable feedback and so much more.

When you look at role models such as Michelle Obama, Oprah Winfrey, Ava DuVernay, Lady Gaga, and Ruth Bader Ginsberg, they all had access to a mentor. Someone who supported them with their ambitions to reach to the next level. With this essay, I want to inspire you to amplify your career through mentorship.

What is mentoring?

Mentoring is a positive, supportive relationship, encouraging mentees to develop to their fullest potential, both personally and professionally. A mentor typically shares their knowledge, experience, and advice with their mentee.

Mentors are trusted advisors and good role models; people who have 'been there, done that'. By providing general and explicit ideas and details, they encourage and support their mentees. The goal is to enhance the abilities of mentees and, ideally, to advance their professional career.

A mentoring relationship can occur between two people working for the same company or industry, but this isn't necessary. The mentor and mentee should always build the mentorship based on mutual respect and confidentiality.

Mentoring and coaching

Mentors and coaches will all support their mentees/coachees to grow personally and professionally. Mentoring and coaching have some parallels and some differences.

A mentor can help you figure out where you are, where you need to go, and how to move forward in your career. A mentor can also assist you to progress towards your goal.

Mentoring differs considerably from coaching in three critical ways. Firstly, a mentorship can have the potential to last a lifetime. Once you have a good connection with your mentor, you may reach out to them in the future. Due to the personal and informal nature of mentoring, it tends to continue for longer than coaching.

Secondly, the mentee is the one who sits in the driver's seat of the bus. The mentee is responsible for driving the sessions and steering the mentorship. Sometimes, people misinterpret that a mentor will tell you what you need to do and shape you into following your ideal journey; the truth is that a mentor does the opposite. The mentee's task is to be dedicated to their professional development and a mentor will support the mentee to achieve their goals. In coaching, the coach is driving the agenda for the relationship. This is rooted in the fact that coaching is more performance related.

Thirdly, in a mentorship, a mentee has specific needs. They need to discuss the challenges they face, so it does not have to be tied to company-wide, top-down performance initiatives. In coaching, the organization identifies a specific skill gap and a coach is selected to provide a program to make improvements. The content is mostly generalized and reused.

Benefits for the mentor

You can also consider becoming a mentor yourself. This will boost your personal and professional skills, by encouraging you to do the following:

- **Build your leadership skills:** It strengthens your ability to inspire and support others. This will motivate you to become a better manager, employee, and co-worker.
- **New perspectives:** Learn new perspectives from your mentee, as the two of you don't speak a common language. Your mentee may have a different background or different experiences. Still, you may find you can learn how to communicate more effectively by exploring the mentorship.
- **Advance your career:** Improving your initiative-taking skills will improve your professional growth; it might help you achieve your promotion. It is becoming increasingly important for success in today's business world to lead like an inclusive leader. Mentorship can be a valuable ingredient for you to be seen as an inclusive leader.
- **Gain personal satisfaction:** It is highly satisfactory to recognize you have contributed directly to someone's growth and success. As a result of your support, it is a reward in itself, which also benefits your mentee.

Benefits For The Mentee

A dedicated and supportive guide will help you to do this with:

- **Primary motivation:** Mentors can provide valuable insights into the choice of your discussion points. A mentor can act like a 'sounding board' for your thoughts, to help you in challenging situations. You will learn different approaches, which can help you work even better, stop you from 'wasting time', or prevent you from taking the wrong turn.

- **Build your experiences and knowledge:** A mentor can help you appreciate your hidden and visible skills and talents, which you can use for amplifying your career. They can provide you with what you need to know or inspire you to find the information you need.
- **Strengthen your relationships:** Like with your mentor, you can also find out how to connect with others, which can also benefit you at work.
- **Learn different insights:** Your mentor can show you other methods for your professional growth. Don't forget, your mentor is learning from you as well.
- **Amplify your career:** A mentor can help you stay focused in your career through skills development, advice, networking, and so on.
- **Develop your skills:** Your mentor can allow you to expand your personal branding within the company and externally.

How do you find a mentor?

Where do you need to start when you want to find a mentor who can help you amplify your career? Here are ten tips to help you identify the right mentor for you and set yourself up for a successful mentorship.

1. Be clear on why and when you want a mentor. Are you looking for a role model to offer specific advice? Or are you looking for a sounding board? Before you even consider approaching your potential mentor, you need to think about what you want to learn and get out of the mentorship. Your mentorship goal should be to help you overcome a challenge, so you can excel in your professional career.

2. Define your personality and communication style. What kind of mentor would be excellent support for you to reach your goal? You may choose someone who's your opposite (i.e., an introvert if you are an extravert). Or go for someone who might give a different perspective and teach you new skills.

3. Before approaching your potential mentor, you need to be able to explain why you're asking them, and what you expect out of the

mentorship. Name your reasons for approaching this particular role model. Do some investigation by going through their LinkedIn profile to have something flattering to share, such as: "I'm asking you, because you are a true inspiration in XYZ area. I want to learn from a person like you!"

4. Before approaching your potential mentor, consider first merely asking for their input on a single specific topic. Did your mentor provide you with some good advice? Was the advice delivered in a way that made sense to you?

5. Reach out and work on the relationship. Invite your potential mentor for a (virtual) coffee and have a conversation about your work and some of the hurdles you are facing. Through this conversation, you will find out if the potential mentor is the right mentor for you. If the potential mentor is not someone you already know, try asking a mutual contact to introduce you to the potential mentor. It can help with the relationship.

6. Be humble and show gratitude. Never let your mentor feel they are taken for granted! Try to provide feedback and share when something did work out for you. A mentor would love to hear how they played an impactful role in your success story. Know that your mentor has a personal and professional life, so show your respect by not claiming all of their time. Find ways to demonstrate your gratitude and kindness.

7. When you are looking for a mentor, think beyond former managers and teachers. Look into a community of leaders, the networks of your friends and co-workers, or network associations you belong to. Avoid asking your direct manager at work. You want to be free to talk about workplace issues, as well as your plans for the potential future career moves you want to make.

8. Keep in mind that mentoring can take place in various forms. It can be a bi-weekly virtual call, a monthly lunch, a quarterly meetup, a weekly squash game or merely a WhatsApp engagement. Thanks

to the internet, your mentor does not even have to live in the same country or city, but it sometimes helps to have face-to-face meetings.

9. Know that a mentor is there to give you a boost, so you can amplify your career, but a mentor will not just give you a handout. Don't start the mentorship with the expectation your mentor will hand things to you on a silver platter.

10. When you ask a potential mentor to become your mentor and this person refuses, don't be offended by it. Know that this is not personal; good mentors are very busy people. Thank them for the consideration and ask if they know someone who would be an ideal mentor for you.

Mentoring has opened a lot of doors for me and inspired me to activate my inner mentorship/sponsorship.

A Call to Action!

Make sure you boost your career through mentoring! I wish you the best of luck with finding your ideal mentor or mentee who can help you with amplifying your career.

Share your mentorship successes and/or challenges with me by connecting with me on LinkedIn.

4

Charlotte Heilmann

***Charlotte Heilmann** helps to negotiate and close commercial deals, while limiting the overall legal risks for the company.*

She is a multi-lingual international commercial lawyer who brings more than 10 years of experience in the software business and private sector, handling many cases and negotiations with regards to competition, software licensing, and intellectual property rights.

She grew up in Germany, spent her legal studies and clerkship in Germany, Belgium, and Luxembourg, and now lives in The Netherlands with her husband and son.

→ *To contact Charlotte: linkedin.com/in/charlotte-heilmann/*

This Is a Man's World...

The universities at which we study, our first job, those in the higher ranks of the corporate structure, and the people who represent us politically, all have an effect on how we see ourselves. Maybe also on how we behave and the goals we set for ourselves.

I wasn't consciously thinking about the beginning of James Brown's song as I started writing this essay. However, it very much summarizes the impression of my educational and professional experience in the legal sector. I was mainly educated by male professors and judges. Often, I've been the only woman in legal negotiations. Regularly, I'm one of two or three women in a larger group of male colleagues in business meetings.

When starting my legal studies in 2003 in Germany, all professors teaching at the two universities I attended were men. Once, I was lucky to meet a female professor, who was introduced by another student as "oh, she probably doesn't see her children very often." Perversely, this representation of the teaching personnel was not reflected in the number of female law students: 48% of the law students in 2003[1] were female. This has been increasing, to women representing 57% of the 119 285 law students in Germany who started in the winter of 2020/2021[2].

I was surrounded by a majority of men: as professors, judges, prosecutors, and as colleagues. This was also my professional experience during my master studies in The Netherlands and legal clerkship in different countries. I received support from all of them. I also learned much in terms of legal knowledge, dedication, and professionalism. However, I realized much later that I missed seeing someone like me in such a position. Someone to whom I could relate to, compare myself to and, most importantly, use as a role model.

Once I started working, I often felt my input would not be valued or what I had to contribute wasn't intelligent enough. An example is how, during a team meeting, a male colleague presented the very same thought I had; only, I had been too afraid to share it. I realized then that my thought was smart, but I was holding myself back to state it in front of the group. All such small and daily experiences fueled my willingness to improve. I became more self-confident, let my voice be heard and slowly corrected my underlying image of women in the workplace.

The importance of role models and networking

Since the beginning of my career, I sought guidance by attending leadership workshops, mentoring, and networking clubs. Not only to share my experiences but also to broaden my views and receive motivation from other professional women.

At work and at such networking clubs, I met a lot of female role models who, amongst other things, corrected my male dominated impression of the legal sector. Role models can help leave manifested images behind, by representing the group to which someone feels connected. They show that dreams and possibilities can be realized.

I was the first person in my family to enter the legal profession. When I entered the work force, it was important to me to find role models. They play a central role in shaping a young professional's career.

The most influential thing that ever happened to me, was working as an in-house legal counsel at international software companies, together with female colleagues and managers. This showed me that the legal sector isn't only led by men. I discovered how I wanted to act and lead in the workplace, and how I didn't. Having strong leading women as colleagues and managers helped me to believe in my own abilities. They helped me to thrive as a legal professional, at an early career stage.

In daily contract negotiations my counterparts are often male, holding positions in sales, procurement, business, or legal. In such situations, I realize that I am in the minority. Nevertheless, it's about the job and it's important to deliver valuable contributions: offering clarifications and engaging with the other party to come to a solution which is satisfying for both, while limiting the risk for the company. I learned that sometimes people may have underlying sentiments and need to receive the message from a man, who they may associate with more power. In the corporate world, it's not unusual to include your manager or another colleague who can support your message into a conversation. I learned to not be afraid to ask for help from a colleague or even a manager. Often, if a colleague, male or female, can repeat the very same message, it becomes sticky and more convincing.

By providing a template of success, role models may also help to shape goals and visualize career aspirations. When starting to work in the Dutch market, I didn't know many role models in the legal sector, especially not many with a non-Dutch legal background. Joining an international women's network, such as the Professional Women Network Netherlands, further strengthened my self-confidence. It also assisted me in visualizing which career paths in the Netherlands were possible. The network, and its welcoming members, provided a safe place to discuss questions such as: how to apply for a job in The Netherlands; how to negotiate a salary increase; how to react to discriminating comments from colleagues; and even the not so simple question of how to manage your personal and professional life. Joining the network and meeting such enthusiastic women assisted my arrival in The Netherlands. It has enabled me to accept my internationality and German legal background as something special, which should actually be emphasized and not hidden. The network provides a pool of female role models outside my work environment, to whom I can relate.

It can start with small steps

Over the years, I learned that not only networks but also each woman plays a role in achieving gender parity and more inclusion in the workplace.

For example, changing your mindset to a more risk-taking approach, allowing you to get out of your comfort zone and not to limit yourself. This could mean speaking up and presenting your idea in a meeting. Or starting a new job which might first have looked like a huge step forward but may conflict with your wish to start a family. Sometimes, I feel that women choose certain studies, sectors, and jobs because they associate them with the possibility to integrate work and private life better. This is, of course, a very valid consideration to make. The COO of Facebook, Sheryl Sandberg, describes preparation for such a potential situation in her book 'Lean In', in the chapter 'Don't leave before you leave'. Not doing proper preparation for future situations may prevent women from pursuing other jobs, promotions or working in male dominated fields. Take, for example, someone who stays in a company without growth opportunities. Or someone else who cuts back on their weekly working hours without having a partner or children.

In the workplace, women could further support and help each other. When speaking about other women, talk about their achievements in your team. Or state how much value they bring to the workplace. In meetings, repeat their message, if you agree with it, making it 'stick' through repetition. And if you don't have anything positive to say about a woman, don't say anything at all. As Former secretary of state Madeleine Albright said in 2016, when introducing Hillary Clinton at an event: "There's a special place in hell for women who don't help each other!"

Further, you could recommend a woman out of your network for an open job position. Remain available for conversations around career opportunities in the company you work in or for members of your network. When hiring, companies need to have a diverse talent pool to choose from. This makes the workplace more diverse and inclusive for all sexes. As a female employee, start increasing and adding to the talent pool your company is hiring from. Supportive activities among women are essential to create a more diverse workplace.

All these 'small' steps are ways we can achieve a more equal representation of gender at schools, universities, workplace, politics, and in the world at large. In addition, by being role models with regards to our own behavior, personally and professionally, we support other women in achieving career success.

A Call to Action!

Luckily, James Brown's lyrics don't end with the first sentence but continue on to express a sentiment fundamental to our society. So too, should our overall journey for parity and equality in the workplace, family, and society. Give woman and girls a seat at the table, representing their interests and ideas. Networks such as the international Professional Women's Network play a substantial role in achieving this.

What will be your next small step to achieving gender parity?

"This is a man's world
This is a man's world
But it would be nothing, nothing
Without a woman or a girl"

Footnotes

[1] Statistisches Bundesamt (Destatis), 2021 | Stand: 24.09.2021
[2] Statistisches Bundesamt (Destatis), 2021 | Stand: 24.09.2021

5

Yulia Yavid

Yulia Yavid *is a Director in Global Transportation & Logistics team of ABN AMRO, Amsterdam. As part of her role, Yulia is responsible for managing EMEA shipping portfolio of ABN AMRO.*

Prior to joining ABN AMRO, Yulia worked at Deloitte Restructuring Services and Amsterdam Trade Bank as a Restructuring Officer. She has more than nine years of experience in banking and financial advisory. Yulia completed her studies in the VU Amsterdam, and the International Banking Institute, St. Petersburg.

Originally from St. Petersburg, Yulia worked and lived in Luxembourg for some time before settling in Amsterdam. Through her career, Yulia gained international experience in a number of sectors including shipping, global and distribution logistics, energy and natural resources, and the oil and gas industry.

Yulia is a passionate advocate of gender equality. She fosters female leadership in Finance by providing coaching and career support for young female talents.

→ *To contact Yulia: linkedin.com/in/yulia-yavid*

The Importance of Financial Intelligence

An historical point of interest happened one sunny day in Paris. I was enjoying a walk with a friend of mine. Trees along the boulevards had just started to bloom and the first rays of the spring sun kept us warm. My friend shared: "In France, women were only given the right to open a bank account in their own name in 1965. Before then, the account had to be in their husband's name. Women also had no right to exercise professional activities without the permission of their families." We both laughed at these facts; they sounded so ridiculous to the two of us.

My friend didn't mean to blame France for its conservative approach towards women's rights. Thanks to French conservatism, sometimes peremptory, we still enjoy one of the best cheese and wine traditions in human history. But in 2021, the thought that women would have no access to a bank account or not be financially independent, was ludicrous. Like some random trivia facts you come across on the internet: that the first computer was the size of a house or that heroin was used as cough medicine. Nowadays, my computer fits in my palm. I don't use anything more aggressive than honey and hot milk to cure my coughs. And I surely have some (maybe too many) credit cards with my name on them.

Today, hardly anyone will argue that a woman isn't capable of making her own financial decisions or even being a frontrunner in the financial industry. There is plenty of research and many examples around the world evidencing this.

Defining the problem

In defiance of academic research, at any financial conference the disproportion of the male versus female audience is obvious. Even the most popular financial newspaper in the world fails to attract a female audience: merely a quarter of the Financial Times' readers are women.[1] The Financial Times concluded this is caused by the failure to provide female oriented materials and appointed Roula Khalaf as a new editor. I applaud such a move. However, I can't accept the argument that women can only digest an adapted piece of information. In my university class, we had 80 women to 50 men studying financial management. We all had the same study materials; none were adapted to suit a certain gender. But at what moment did 60% of female finance students became 'merely a quarter'?

To me the answer is clear: it's not the education that is a showstopper but a lack of confidence and financial intelligence. According to Eurostat, 44% of women have a post-secondary education degree or higher, compared to 34% of men.[2] A woman can be better educated and still believe her spouse is better equipped to invest family money. Women find themselves less interested in reading news, cautious of making major financial decisions, and tend to rely on their spouses for investments. When I asked my friends 'who has access to the family investment account?', a significant number of them failed to respond affirmatively.

This is what I see as the core problem: women tend to underestimate the importance of financial intelligence and don't realize the long-term consequences of doing so.

Why is financial intelligence so important?

In researching for this essay, I found examples of women who had neglected the importance of developing their financial intelligence.

By doing so, they put themselves in a difficult, if not hopeless position, without even realizing it. What was most eye-opening, was to discover all the scary statistics behind these stories.

Starting a career

A few years ago, while working for an international financial institution, I had a chance to hire Anna, a young female university graduate, for an intern position. I chose her from many applicants because of the extensive experience she had, despite her young age. With her volunteer work, a business on Instagram, and an active investment account, Anna had it all. She was very diligent in her role, completing her tasks accurately and on time. There wasn't a day I regretted hiring her. That is why I was happy to recommend Anna for a permanent position in the company.

Imagine my surprise when her application was rejected after the first round of interviews. Anna had no clue about the company she worked for. She wasn't up to speed with the industry developments and not aware of the major market players. She couldn't name key management players and even the organizational structure was not familiar to her. Her knowledge of the company was clearly the bare minimum of what she required to manage her daily tasks. At the time of the interview, no-one in the interview process knew her. She had no network and decision makers were not aware of her achievements.

When the next applicant came in, everyone in the room knew him very well. He was not the most diligent employee and certainly not the most hardworking one. Nevertheless, everyone knew him as someone who is always active at the conferences; the guy who made that funny joke at corporate events and someone with whom you can have an interesting talk with at lunch. In just six months, he'd managed to make a good impression across the entire organization. His application got unanimous support without any discussion.

We actually hired them both. When I handed Anna her job offer, she couldn't believe her eyes. She rushed to sign the employment agreement as if she thought that it'd disappear, should she hesitate. She never attempted to negotiate her salary. With the second applicant, a completely different situation occurred. He asked me if he could have a day to consider his options. He returned with a counteroffer and, after some discussion, managed to get a slightly higher salary.

It was a minuscule difference between his and Anna's salary. Just like the gender wage gap of $0.99 for young female professionals under 29, becoming $0.98 when they turn 30. It will become $0.76 to every $1.00 earned by men, if both of them complete an MBA program and will grow even bigger if they make Finance or Legal their careers. More than 50% of female professionals earn less than their male peers. Eventually, it evolves into an unsurmountable wage gap at the executive level[3]. It always starts with a one cent difference we accept at the very start of our careers, even though nobody asked us to.

The story of my former co-worker serves as an illustration of the recent report of the EU commission on the female labor market. Anna managed to hit all three attention points of that report, becoming an example of what the EU calls "challenges of women's participation in the labor market, pay and earnings gaps."

A perfect mother

Claire and I started our careers on the same day, fresh from university. A few years later, we both had promising careers and fair chances for a promotion. Neither of us believed in gender inequality and we were confident in our powers, like no man in the room.

When she had her first baby, she assessed all the pros and cons and decided to work part-time for a while. That was the moment she joined "one third (31.4%) of women in employment in the EU working on a part-time basis."[4] Her husband, again in complete alignment with the statistics, continued working fulltime, as 92% of young fathers do.[5]

A few years later, my friend had her second baby and life suddenly became more expensive. Her part-time salary couldn't justify the cost of day care and the only sensible solution was to quit her job and become a stay-at-home mother. That's the day she hit another statistical group: "50% of the potential female workforce (aged 25-49) are inactive because women are looking after children."[6]

One could say she made the right financial decision. If day care is more expensive than what you earn, it makes sense to stop working and take care of your children. Adding up the savings like lunch expenses, occasional nanny's, and cleaning costs makes it sound even more sensible. But is it?

When making such a financial decision, women mainly focus on the short-term horizon, overlooking the long-term consequences of leaving work. Making such decisions based on today's salary means missing all the potential upsides one could have as a working mom. These include salary raises, promotions, performance bonuses, and most importantly: avoiding the salary cut when re-entering the job market after an extended maternity leave. These are the elements most often overlooked when a decision is made. And this is where my friend gets close to the last, most scary statistical group.

Women tend to have lower pension contributions, resulting in higher pension gaps (approximately 40%),[7] putting them at greater risk of poverty or social exclusion after retirement. This is a result of differences in their work experience due to lower employment levels, the type of jobs, the high prevalence of part-time work, and part-time work being associated with significantly lower hourly wages

Women can easily avoid unnecessary financial stress in the future by making a wise financial decision today.

A good wife

The final story is about my university classmate, Diane. Diane graduated with distinction from university with a dual degree in Finance. She was recruited by a large international firm right after graduation and had a prosperous financial career in front of her.

When she married, her husband was running a small IT business. Diane decided to leave her current job and support her spouse. After 10 years of marriage, the small family business grew into a successful franchise. It no longer required her daily involvement and she decided to step down to pursue her passion for baking. One year later, they divorced. The divorce brought several unpleasant surprises with it.

Firstly, she was never a co-owner of the family business. It was registered under her spouse's name. On paper, she was an employee with a fixed salary like every other employee in the company. It never appeared as a problem before. There was never a distinction between his and her money; they were a family, after all.

Secondly, all the family property was registered either to the company or in her husband's name. At first glance, Diana and her husband looked to be equal partners but on paper she was completely financially dependent on him.

Even though she was a finance professional, she let her husband take care of all the financial decisions. He arranged the investment account and took care of the mortgage. Even the electric bills were registered in his name. Despite having a financial background and working in the financial sector herself for over a decade, she had no control over her own money.

Even during her divorce, she never attempted to negotiate for herself. She fully relied on her spouse to take care of all the financial matters, even if they were not in her best interest. I believe she left the marriage with two suitcases, a vase and full confidence in how it had been handled.

She is not alone in her struggles. Nearly half of women worldwide (49%) defer long-term financial decisions to their spouses, putting their future financial security at risk[8]. Which results in even less pleasant statistics evidenced by the overwhelming number of women (74%) discovering negative financial surprises after a divorce[9].

Different but the same

Though completely different circumstance, all three women made the same mistake: they neglected the importance of financial intelligence in their lives. Large or small, their decisions had a huge impact on their future. Had they taken one small step towards being financially intelligent about their own lives, each of them could have prevented this impact.

A Call to Action!

It is not easy to develop financial intelligence and make it an integral part of your life. Like every other skill, it requires practice. Realize the importance of it and dare to take responsibility of your own finances. Stop thinking that somebody else will take better care of your money than you. Educate yourself, read the news and explore which areas of finance are most alluring to you. Be ready to stand for your financial independence and think of what you can achieve with self-confidence. And most importantly, be vocal about your achievements, so women around you will be inspired by your example.

Footnotes

[1] Interview with Head of Digital Editorial Development at the Financial Times and Assistant Editor https://www.niemanlab.org/2018/04/if-the-financial-times-were-a-person-it-would-be-a-man-heres-how-the-paper-is-trying-to-change-that/

[2 4 5 6 7] European Semester Thematic Factsheet Women In The Labour Market https://ec.europa.eu/info/sites/default/files/european-semester_thematic-factsheet_labour-force-participation-women_en_0.pdf

[3] www.payscale.com: The State of the Gender Pay Gap in 2021 https://www.payscale.com/data/gender-pay-gap#section06

[8] UBS research https://www.ubs.com/global/en/media/display-page-ndp/en-20200706-key-to-gender-equality.html

[9] UBS research https://www.ubs.com/global/en/media/display-page-ndp/en-20190306-financial-security.html

6

Béatrice Blondiau

Béatrice Blondiau *is a champion of positivity and adaptability. She believes in the power of self-knowledge, continuous learning, authentic communication, and people connections. As a black African woman, she grew up in disadvantageous environments, embracing fears, and high levels of stress.*

She studied business engineering and has an affinity for foreign languages (she speaks 5 languages, of which 3 fluently). Her career spans 20 years in the IT industry.

Béatrice knows that being a minority in a white, male, Anglo-Saxon dominated business environment is not easy, not only for women but for anyone being different.

Next to her work in IT, she has become a sophrologist, helping employees and leaders to reach balance in life by: developing greater self-awareness, becoming more courageous, cultivating an optimistic attitude, and gaining in vitality. Béatrice believes that happy people can create more diverse and inclusive environments. Ultimately, they can contribute to a better world.

→ *To contact Béatrice: linkedin.com/in/beatriceblondiau-teaching-positivity-at-work*

Trust Your Own Capacities and Realize Your Potential

What do you know about the strength of a disabled person who wants to contribute to society? What do you know about the courage of a man who wants to communicate and act differently from his male peers? What do you know about the perseverance of a woman who wants it all: a family, a career, and a legacy?

A call for more authenticity: show up, just as you are!

If you are part of a minority, you might know how it feels to be different, to stand out from the crowd. For many years, as a black African woman, I didn't have the courage to stand for who I am. Instead, to conform and belong, I put myself under huge pressure to acquire degrees and competencies, yearning to belong and to experience success. This strategy was a mistake, affecting my self-confidence, wasting my real capabilities, and my vision of myself for the future. But the story is not finished. It is only the beginning; and there is HOPE!

'Fake it until you make it' sucks

Coming from a minority position, there is a strong inclination to catch up on what might be perceived as a deficit. There may be an urgent need to look for any means to blur the differences. Why? To fulfill an essential human need of love and belonging[1]. When it comes to career, to be accepted by the group becomes a question of survival; it is your ticket to fulfill two of our fundamental needs: safety and physiological.

Luckily, not everyone who stands out for being different reacts this way! Unfortunately, it is how I behaved for 40 years, wasting my own talents and draining energy I could have dedicated to better causes. During this chapter of my life, I felt very lonely and uncomfortable (day and night!). My real potential was jeopardized. Thanks to the lessons I have learned from two burnouts and earning a degree in sophrology[2], I see two axes to influence things positively: the environment and the person himself/herself suffering from a minority position.

Let's start with the attitude to adopt in order to bypass the pain I went through for not feeling 'enough' and rather ashamed for being who I am: a black African Woman.

Unconditional self-acceptance

First of all, this is a question of personal leadership. I was leaving my fate in the hands of others. No matter how unfair and inequitable an environment may be, I needed to realize I was responsible for the situation I was in. And therefore, it was a change in my behavior that would get me unstuck. I needed to wake up! The nice little fairy godmother doesn't exist. Once I understood the good as well as the bad stemming from my own behavior, I was able to get out from the position as a victim of a minority. Important conditions to this process are self-love and humility. I learned not to be hard on myself and not take myself too seriously. I became my own BFF, with a great sense of humor, able to experience self-forgiveness, allow myself to heal when it hurts and, in the end, to laugh out loud. We tend to take our feelings and ourselves much too seriously; so much so that sometimes we forget the earth keeps rotating, with or without us.

Self-love: respecting yourself no matter what, listening to your own needs and aspirations, is one of the main pillars for building self-esteem.

"Self-esteem is made of [a] balanced and interdependent mix of self-love, which nurtures a positive vision of ourselves (a belief in own capacities, positive projection of ourselves in the future) and in turn consolidates self-confidence (act without unnecessary fear of failure and the judgment of others."[3]

With a higher self-esteem, decisions are easier and quicker, while daring to take more risks. These are important qualities successful leaders and entrepreneurs possess. Our (work or private life) environment can either make or break our self-confidence and capacity to pursue our own agenda and priorities, if we allow it. It is in our power to practice self-love and spend more time to build, maintain and grow a supportive network. This helps to nurture a more positive vision of ourselves, which we need in order to accomplish our goals and ambitions.

Not feeling enough: a terrible vicious circle

During my childhood and adolescence, there was no room for self-love, neither at school nor at home. Achieving high results, becoming wealthy, and creating safety were far more important than dealing with feelings and self-love. Numbers and ranking were the only ways in which I felt valued by the people in my environment. Growing up in the 80's as a black African girl in the Belgian countryside, I had always been a singular minority at school. In that period of my life, wanting desperately to conform and belong to a group, I fit in nowhere. I felt terribly misplaced and ashamed with my wild, frizzy hair and a skin that felt as if it was too dark. With conservative parents from a post-colonial age, I was surrounded by a mix of cultures of Congolese food, music, and social structure from my mother and French-Belgian art, music, and gastronomy tastes from my father. I was a melting pot of these, all of which didn't match with anybody at school. To belong, I had to constantly learn and adapt quickly. To break the biases and preconceptions Belgian people had about people coming from Congo, and later to counter racist judgements, I was convinced I had to get a prestigious job to climb up in society. A good job was, in my eyes, my ticket to improve my own social condition and that of my family.

With time going by, looking back at the movie of my own life experience, I can say today that self-esteem cannot only rest on competencies. For a very long period, I have been trapped in a vicious circle of continuous learning, feeding a feeling of 'never knowing enough'. For many years I worked hard, very hard, to perform at work and at home, repeating the same mistakes of my parents; my days were full of actions to be completed and there wasn't much time left for feelings, nor for spontaneous love to give or receive from others, and even less time for myself. Instead, although surrounded by friends, a loving partner, and three wonderful children, I felt terribly lonely and even more inefficient and incompetent. I worked even harder, to finally collapse, exhausted and burned out.

The value of safe spaces

My work environment was toxic at that time and my family didn't understand my daily challenges. I didn't give them much opportunity to understand, since I was controlling and organizing everything for everybody! I was responsible for the situation I was in. I didn't set my boundaries. I didn't listen to signals of personal urgent needs. I didn't love myself enough.

At work, a supportive care team helped me get back on track and make practical decisions for a better work-life balance. Despite the support, patience, and understanding of my colleagues, it wasn't at work that I started to rebuild self-confidence and a higher self-esteem. It was outside the work and family sphere.

Indeed, in December 2017, something special happened when I decided to participate in a network event dedicated to professional working women. During that evening, for the first time in a professional context, I felt welcomed for who I was. I didn't have to feel ashamed of my condition; people were sincerely curious to know about me and were naturally supportive. During this 2-3 hour-event, I recognized fears and challenges I was still suffering from or had overcome. In the latter case, I was able to share my experience to support a fellow sister. Also, I was inspired by success stories from others, demonstrating that success is not limited to high scores or degrees. Achievements are relative and can have so many shapes and cover so many aspects. On that day, in the eyes of strangers, I started to see my own value.

My success formula: (ME x NETWORK) + TIME = SUCCESS (or Hope!)

With my story, I hope I have made clear how important self-love and a professional welcoming network are in developing higher self-esteem. Relying on ranking and degrees seriously damaged the vision I had about myself. When I carried with me curiosity and (even hidden!) talents, an ambitious network of like-minded professionals helped me unleash my real capacities and self-confidence. Through the eyes of others, I became aware of my real value. This can only be realized in a place where one feels welcome and safe, and where the feedback that is given is honest and constructive. Places like these are a safe harbor to come back to because shame and guilt don't have a place there.

Do you feel the HOPE now? It's all in your hands

Since the day two cells merged to create the unique individual that you have become today, you have deserved the right to exist and contribute on this planet. No matter the conditions you were born into or the traumas you have experienced, there is something precious in you that no one can take away from you. Success is not a question of performances; first you need to feel successful with yourself, from deep within. Our achievements, and probably even more our failures and our scars, contribute to the value of our uniqueness.

A Call to Action!

In the end, it is our responsibility to embrace this uniqueness for the good of the world. It requires strength, courage, and perseverance but also a large piece of self-love to face our authenticity. As a minority, don't put yourself under pressure as I did, feeling the urgency to catch up to the detriment of your uniqueness. Please, don't stay alone and instead look for a group of cheerleader peers where you feel welcome, understood, and supported and who can lift you up as a minority.

You are enough with who you are; keep the faith in your own capacities. Someone in this world needs you.

Footnotes

1 Maslow's hierarchy of needs is a theory of motivation which states that five categories of human needs dictate an individual's behavior. Those needs are physiological needs, safety needs, love and belonging needs, esteem needs, and self-actualization needs. https://www.masterclass.com/articles/a-guide-to-the-5-levels-of-maslows-hierarchy-of-needs#what-are-the-5-levels-of-maslows-hierarchy-of-needs

2 Sophrology was created by Professor Caycedo, a Spanish neuropsychiatrist (1932-2017) in 1960 to study consciousness and propose a method to live a more balanced and joyful life. Sophrology means "the study of consciousness in harmony". The method is based on practical easy-to-do exercises developed by Caycedo in specific protocols that a Caycedian sophrologist will teach to help people develop self-awareness, self-confidence and positive healthy habits. The method addresses all aspect of work and life like stress, burn-out prevention, insomnia, exams preparation, sport performances, birth, etc. and is recognized in countries like Belgium, France, Spain or Switzerland to improve health recovery.

3 L'Estime de soi – S'aimer pour mieux vivre avec les autres» Christophe André et François Lelor (Ed. Odile Jacob)

7

Janine Khuc

Janine Khuc *is a passionate, machine learning engineer/data scientist. She is curious about what the world could be like. This drives and motivates her in everything she does. She has a background in Psychology and a devoted interest in machine learning applications. With this, she is interested in understanding the human reflection which shows up in the data. She also wants to know how these biases can be mitigated to leverage the potential of data to enable better decision making.*

Intrigued by the intrinsic nature of biases in the way humans think and perceive, Janine is also actively working towards achieving a proportionate gender representation. She encourages, inspires, and promotes minority gender people to achieve their programming potential. She is building their confidence 'on stage' with the local R-Ladies chapter in Amsterdam.

→ *To contact Janine: linkedin.com/in/janine-khuc*

Opening Doors

It's a topic that accompanies me day in and day out: being and working with women in tech. Why is it that I have to specify that it's women? Can't we just have a conversation about people in tech? Sadly, not yet. We all know the scary statistics of the disproportionate representation of men within tech fields. But honestly, why do we, as a society, miss out on opportunities to innovate, by having only one half of the population develop innovations for all of us?

My story started out as an opportunity; an idea to provide space for others to connect, support and learn from one another. It turned out to be so much more.

In this essay I'd like to share what can happen when you remove some of the fog created by self-limiting thoughts. To give yourself a chance to listen to the spark within you; those small things each of us can do for ourselves and others. So, this will be a tale about how I ventured into the world of data science to help others, like me, find a place where we feel we belong.

Where I started

It all started with me studying Psychology, as I have always been incredibly intrigued by the ins and outs of human existence; our ability to learn, innovate, and create. While I did enjoy these studies, I quickly discovered that I was constantly pulled towards statistics and methodology: the question of exactly how the authors got to their conclusions. I never liked to purely rely on the conclusions of others but enjoyed discovering 'the why' for myself, supported by other people's ideas.

As the seeds of statistics, data, and methodology were planted in my head, I soon considered the idea to move towards something that sounded like a pure buzzword back then: data science. I knew it had something to do with data and that's what I wanted to do. I started to get my head around the idea of programming, first discovering a programming language that was mostly used within research and statistics called R. By venturing into this land of programming myself, I soon also discovered there was an entire community behind it. One of those communities I came across was R-Ladies global; a global diversity initiative wanting to encourage, inspire, and empower underrepresented minorities within the R-community. The goal is to achieve a proportionate representation within the community. I came across a chapter in London, where I was living at the time. Joining the first event, I was inspired by the energy, the support, and inspiration all R-ladies gave one another. I had not experienced such a great support network before, as I had never realized it was needed to separate by gender.

Entering the uncomfortable

When I was accepted to continue my journey into the data world, I moved to Amsterdam. I hoped to join the R-community events to benefit from them, to give me energy and connect within a city that was so new to me. It was exciting and scary at the same time. After moving to Amsterdam, I learned there wasn't a R-ladies chapter here. As coincidence would have it, I was introduced to the idea of organizing events myself.

The idea excited me: to be able to support others coming together, creating an inspirational space which gives energy. At the same time, it seemed daunting. In my head were thoughts that might sound familiar to some: *'I had just learned how to code myself half a year ago. How could I teach anyone else?' 'I've never organized an event before. What would be all the things I'd have to consider?' 'What would it involve to find sponsors?'* I thought I was bad at small talk; was afraid of talking to strangers. How could I do all those things I felt were reserved for all those super shiny, bubbly extroverts out there?

The thoughts didn't stop there but continued. Until finally I reached a point when I realized these were just my own thoughts holding me back. What was I really afraid of? What was the worst thing that could happen? I'd fail, would be judged, and no one would be interested in these kinds of events. But would it really be that bad? We encounter so many people on a daily basis. Do we really always remember everyone who experienced failure in a negative light? Not really; we are all preoccupied with our own lives. So, if no-one will be judging me, why am I making it so hard for myself? All those inspiring stories out there. What's the core to them? People telling stories of struggles and how they conquered them. What about if it could be a learning opportunity? What's the best thing that could happen?

I felt this little spark in me that had been difficult to discover because of all the noisy thoughts. I liked the idea of creating only a fraction of the atmosphere I previously experienced. Maybe I'd be able to enable one or two people to connect and make a new friend; wouldn't that be enough? It would be very far outside of my comfort zone but something in me said yes! Why not? The worst thing that could happen is not even that bad!

The starting of R-Ladies Amsterdam

The global R-Ladies organization is very committed and provides lots of support and information for starting a local chapter. Tess and I were connected through this platform, and we started meeting up, brainstorming about our first event. Our discussions were a rollercoaster of emotions. We were motivated and eager to change the world and frustrated about the lack of women in every role. What hit me the most is that many of our unconscious associations between competency and the male gender come from the lack of female role models and speakers on stage. It was then clear that, in order to tackle this, we'd need female speakers and male and female R-enthusiasts to join the community. It would be a small step, but it would be a step!

The starting days were quite challenging as we had trouble finding speakers. We didn't know how to approach a sponsor or even how to write a formal email. But we quickly got some extra assistance. Two additional organizers crossed our paths who helped us reach out to universities and companies. We supported one another by reading through our email drafts, preparing sponsor meetings together, brainstormed and thought about everything that might be needed.

Luck was on our side. Our first event came together when a company reached out to us. They also had a female speaker for us, who was absolutely thrilled just by our existence, drive, and motivation to change the current landscape. This was something very far out of my understanding back then. How come there was such an interest from companies? As soon as we got in touch with the company, they were incredibly supportive. We had our event, together with a speaker, meeting space, food, and drinks!

As soon as the event was posted online, it was hard for me to believe that we had over 60 people interested in joining us! 60 people! After I doubted whether there would be a handful of people interested. It got even better. During our first event, I was so nervous. I had to give the introduction to the R-ladies which I had practiced for days. But the energy in the room was thrilling. Every single person who joined us was super excited about the community, after Tess and I shared our ideas and dreams for the R-Ladies Amsterdam community. The struggles beforehand had definitely been worth it!

Fast forward

Fast forward three years. I could never have imagined I would do it for such a long time, even in the middle of the pandemic in which we live to the date of this writing (Summer 2021). Pre-pandemic, Tess sadly had to step down after a year. But together we managed to have monthly events, during which we brought the community together. Newbies and organizers came monthly to support and learn from one another. I learned to give presentations myself, got comfortable in welcoming and connecting with strangers, who very soon became friends. I supported speakers in preparing their workshops, both on a technical level and on a personal level. As well, I supported new organizers in finding their niche to help the community grow. The community enabled people, such as myself, to connect with companies and new friends, assisting in finding new opportunities.

Our online community is now about 1000 members, and we went global. Since early 2020, we went online. At first, I was sad about the lack of opportunities for the community to come together physically. Instead of being paralyzed by the situation, like many others we found new ways for our community to connect online, going beyond physical borders. What started out as me wanting a place to feel comfortable, turned out to open up so many doors and opportunities for so many.

I discovered on this journey that my closing off doors with my own thoughts was not something unique to me. Realizing this enabled me to start talking about it and supporting others doing the same. I gained strength through my perceived weakness. Talking about it also enabled others to feel more comfortable and less lonely, whether it was a co-organizer, community member, speaker, a working colleague, or friend.

A Call to Action!

How can you step slightly outside of your comfort zone? What would you like to try but have not dared to do so far? Which doors are you keeping closed out of fear? Next time you are in a situation outside of your comfort zone, don't focus on your failures and things that could go wrong. See it as a learning opportunity; an opportunity to make mistakes, fail and bring forth a new perspective in your own and other people's lives.

8

Sonya Richardson

***Sonya Richardson** is partner with Spark for Growth, a niche consulting firm dedicated to transforming mindset & behaviors by sparking energy for change. With extensive experience in leadership consulting, Sonya supports global clients across industries from banking to technology to professional services.*

She typically works with clients on designing strategic journeys, transforming organizational cultures, strengthening top team effectiveness, and increasing leadership potential. She acts as designer and facilitator of leadership development programs for professional service firms, corporate settings, and within academic institutions (e.g. Nijenrode University, Utrecht University).

As a former PWN Global President, a global network dedicated to accelerating gender balanced leadership, Sonya is a known speaker on leadership and female leadership themes and has presented on multiple stages across the globe (e.g. WIL Dubai, WF Paris, etc.)

To contact Sonya: linkedin.com/in/sonyaarichardson/
→ *sparkforgrowth.com/*

The Strength of Maternal Lineage

Leading others requires leading self, said Seneca back in the 1st century AD. Daniel Goleman repeated that message back in the 90's. Since then, we have seen a proliferation of insights in how emotional intelligence helps drive leadership success. Although this change in leadership has enabled women to thrive, there is still a huge gap between genders in the workplace. The higher ranks are mostly claimed by men.

Surprising, as research shows women outperform men in most of the skills relating to Emotional Intelligence. We now know that unconscious bias is at the core of this gap, with men and women unconsciously preferring men for leadership roles. These biases are being addressed and sometimes remedied in organizations, although progress is slow.

Experience in working with hundreds of professional women shows there is another unconscious element that needs remedying: the power of maternal lineage. This essay captures how the maternal lineage is a strength, but oftentimes becomes more of a burden. What is needed is to allow the maternal lineage to be a driver of professional success for women. And for it not to be an additiona load to the already demanding lives of professional women today.

Great organizations have great leaders. I love helping people become greater leaders. Why? Because greater leaders make for happier and more fulfilling lives and societies. I particularly enjoy helping women become greater leaders. I strongly believe the world today needs more female leadership to realize those happier societies. As long as there is no balanced leadership, we are losing potential. Women in leadership bring enhanced diversity in thinking and more team and development focus, among lots of other skills. As a result, organizations become more successful in every way. Encouraging curiosity and fostering courage are core to this endeavor. With curiosity and courage, anyone is able to accelerate personal and professional growth, in a way that can feel liberating and without limits. This kind of leadership leads to greater places to work and perhaps more importantly, inspires others to lead similarly.

Conscious evaluation of our values and skills

A leadership journey often requires bigger change in our behaviors than most expect. After all, if we are to lead others, we need to lead ourselves. That change can feel tough as it forces us to review our mindsets: the place where our emotions, our values, and our needs are rooted. Particularly in uncovering which values and needs drive our behaviors, we enter into the daunting territory of the unconscious. For those coming up in the ranks, developing these skills gets you a long way. For those further on in their careers and further up the ladder, the key to growth is uncovering that unconsciousness. Only then will you recognize which values and needs are strengths and which are holding you back.

So how do values and needs relate to maternal lineage and, more broadly, what defines so-called intergenerational loyalty? In a nutshell, our desire for sense of purpose is also rooted in aspirations and unfulfilled dreams of our ancestors and not just our own. All of us, men and women, unconsciously carry forward themes from our family generations before us. The science of behavioral epigenetics and systemic thinking is evolving rapidly and teaching us what many of us unconsciously already knew: we are not only living our lives but also of those before us.

In working with men, I notice that they often operate on an automatic pilot that was activated from a very young age. The notion of predictability in their career development is one that resonates constantly. Whether it be a parent, usually the father, who was in the same or a similar role, or the ingrained sense of responsibility of assuming the patriarchal role, for most it comes across as a given. My heart always goes out to those who clearly experience the burden of that destiny. Those who never dared to follow their heart in becoming the artist or the forester, as they unconsciously were destined to become the lawyer, the surgeon, or the CEO.

The female leaders journey

But in all fairness, my heart goes out more to the female leaders. Their journey is more arduous. It requires redefining cultural expectations of them as women, and also acknowledging and addressing unconscious loyalties to previous maternal generations. It is unsurprising that we see so many women step off the corporate ladder, as they enter into their 40s. Whilst putting their hearts fully into their professional roles, they need to work twice as hard as their male colleagues. Often, because of unconscious biases, they are bypassed for leadership roles. Given this context, in 'my books', it is simply heroic for a woman to get a great leadership job done well, whilst juggling family responsibilities at the same time. It's a tall order to fill.

From experience in working with hundreds of female leaders, the unconscious loyalties to their mothers, grandmothers, and beyond are either a driver of professional success or a driver of demise. The distinguishing factor between either success or demise is how conscious and aware women are of their unconscious loyalties to their maternal lineage. With full awareness, it suddenly becomes easier to define and maintain personal boundaries in a way that allows them to thrive professionally.

We're not only talking about how this loyalty unconsciously results in the added demands on the home front. That voice of your mother ringing unconsciously in your head to keep the house tidy, feed the children wholesome meals, have the ironing done, make sure all the social activities are booked into the calendar, etcetera. This voice unconsciously rings louder in women's heads than it does in men's. We're all fully aware of that double burden for women. We're also still a long way off from seeing husbands and partners have an equal share in all the tasks at home. It's time we remedied this burden. We need to break with the concept that it is normal for a mother to work part-time or below her capacity because she unconsciously feels called upon to take on this role at home.

Let's look at how this unconscious loyalty adds more complexity as women define themselves professionally. As women try to rid themselves from an identity that merely provides a perfectly run household, society is also asking women to step up and claim their space in the workplace. Previous generations fought hard to claim a voice in society through voting rights and a voice in business. This took decades of emancipation and feminism movements. Most will remember mothers losing their jobs as they became pregnant or when they got married. Some may also have grandmothers who made it to university but never got a chance to put their great minds to work. Or worse, grandmothers and mothers who weren't allowed to study and hardly had a say in whom they would marry.

Claiming our space

Given such restricted lives in the past, just imagine the unconscious responsibility many women carry today to make many historical wrongs right. In our patriarchal society, women in history have needed to be strong and courageous to claim their own roles. Many of us are descendants of mothers and grandmothers who were unable to achieve their full professional potential. As such, women in our day and age are committed to doing all they can to claim their space. Therefore, we see so much dedication, commitment, and passion in women in their professional roles today. How many are aware that they may be doing so to make their mothers proud or to live their mother's dreams? Consciously and unconsciously, there is a real sense of urgency to break the glass ceiling once and for all.

But what if you are a woman who is living your mother's dream? What if the stakes are so high, and your passion and commitment to your professional life are so urgent, that it becomes a burden to you? Or the personal cost becomes too high, as you haven't been able to rid yourself from the responsibilities at home? A common pattern I have observed, over the past decades in working with female leaders, is that this passion and commitment can thwart the ability to let go. To not be able to accept a less than perfect result; to not see what has been achieved, rather than what has not. If this happens, women suddenly turn into critical mothers in the workplace and leaders who don't attract followers. As a result, they become their own enemies. Those wonderful skills of allowing others to grow and develop, change into being controlling, critical, and demanding.

When women gain a better understanding of their loyalties to previous generations, they can start defining and maintaining boundaries in a way that will help them thrive at limited personal cost. These boundaries need to be embedded in a conscious awareness of their needs and how those have been influenced by generations before them. That's where I see women really start to thrive. It requires recognizing and then uncoupling personal aspiration from those of their mothers, grandmothers and beyond. And in doing so, never losing the strength and power of the maternal lineage, that allows so many great women to prosper and strengthen their courage to become great leaders.

As someone recently described to me so beautifully: "Once I let go of the sense of burden in which I tried to live my mother's dream but instead chose to live my own, I felt liberated. I still relied on the great strength of my mother and grandmother, but now as a source of strength instead of responsibility. It felt like my journey became lighter because I felt less responsible for achieving more than only my destiny. In doing so, I allowed myself more to play and experiment. This lightness helped me thrive at work and I also found that I became a better mother, a better spouse, and a better friend. In the end, it was all about letting go of something that was not mine to carry."

Our current journey is one of becoming more aware and consciously choosing to live only our own lives and not those of past generations. Women may then be freeing themselves to set their own boundaries and thrive in whomever they choose to become. Baby boomers in large part, hardly got to live so consciously. The majority of Generation X started their careers long before they got a chance to reflect on their journey and many still haven't. More insight is needed into the relevance of this conscious stance, combined with a growing critical mass of female leaders and great female role models. The hope is then, that most Millennials and Generation Z will be able to thrive from the start of their careers.

A Call to Action!

Personally, I would love to see my Generation Alpha daughter step into the world of work with nothing to hold her back from living her life. In fact, success would be, if one day she turns around to me and asks why in my lifetime it was so necessary to help great female leaders create and shape even greater professional careers. That her world would be one where female leadership is no longer the challenge it has been for decades and still is today. Will you help make this possible for her and her generation?

9

Pema Nooten

***Pema Nooten** is the founder of the Architect of Happiness and a world class visionary on happiness at work, personal development, and joy in life. Pema has a worldwide network, deep knowledge of the Eastern and Western culture, spirituality, and the art of life. After living and working in Asia, she developed herself as a strategic partner, coach, and inspirator.*

Combining her eastern wisdom on life, with her western knowledge of the corporate world, makes her a valuable happiness expert to transform professionals and entrepreneurs leading their best lives.

→ *To contact Pema: linkedin.com/in/pemanooten*
thearchitectofhappiness.com

Can You Imagine Finding Yourself?

A few years ago, I went to an art gallery where a photo of a little girl, not much older than 5 years old, was on display. The photo of her as an adult merged into one picture. I was looking at two people with a gap of 20 to 30 years; or was it just one?

The photo moved me. It moved me because I could see the journey taken by a little girl growing up into a beautiful woman. And a whole life between them. Apart from these obvious differences, I could also see the dualities in life: Light and Darkness; Big and Small; Pain and Happiness; Movement and Stillness; Past and Future.

There was also something else that moved me. The journey, taken back in time, transported me to places where I once belonged, to cities and places I have visited. It was like navigating through the depths of my memories. I became a traveler of my own history.

I sometimes feel my hand going to touch that younger me in a photo, to comfort her, and to feel the warmth. It's like travelling back in time. My eyes become the passageway to the past, present, and future.

There are many kinds of images and memories, touching on our physical, emotional, and mental realities. They can lead to someplace new or provide a way to find oneself. There are always questions popping up:

- Why was I doing that, at that moment 10 years ago?
- How did I like my coffee 5 years ago?
- What will I be doing 6 years from now?
- What is the purpose of bringing the past, present, and future together?

When I meet this little girl, and I definitely want to, I will ask her many questions. We have so much to tell each other. There are so many lost memories, like fragments, joined together over time. I have to consciously look for them, cherish them, and give them a place. I don't want my memories to be buried. So many have escaped. What do I bring into the light? What does the other you bring into the light? It's a relief to know I am now somewhere specific, that I came from somewhere and there is somewhere to go.

I certainly experienced boundless love and happiness. Travelling over time was like loving beyond boundaries. I am, we are all, interconnected, even over time. My emotions, my searching, represented my younger self. That little girl was able to send love to the present me. That girl is essentially another version of myself. We are deeply connected, my younger version and me. Going to my younger self unleashed a shower of love. A vast emotion, that had been hidden, was set free in my unconsciousness and in my mind. Now it was able to travel boundlessly. It was like coming home from my travels.

We all know that journeys are challenging, leaving a familiar home and entering new territory. There were many moments in my life when I didn't know what to do or where to go. Embarking on a journey of love and happiness is like this; it can feel scary. Maybe it's fear of getting lost and not being able to find the way forward or back.

On this self-discovery journey, it's possible to get stuck and stay in one place. It's also possible to be swept along so rapidly that one loses their bearings. We need something that gives us a sense of direction and room to explore and grow. The path is like any journey into unchartered territory. We need a picture of a younger self and a guide to reach our destination. But we also need to examine our perception of ourselves, our actions, and the world around us.

What someone does is not the same as who someone is. Our seemingly solid self is, in fact, not all that solid. Our sensations and experiences rise and fall continually. Questions and doubts arise about that hidden treasure of love and happiness. What is needed for more clarity?

- Find and trust a good guide
- Become aware of limiting beliefs and thoughts
- Expand horizons
- Love more inclusively with compassion
- Start noticing our reactions to others in our daily life
- Look more deeply into your actions and habits and their consequences
- Examine the attitudes and actions of our encounters with others

On every journey, circumstances and people will be attracted. With a guide, other attitudes and actions arise; rapport is built. Intimacy starts looking around the corner, resulting in a connection with the person. This is real contact, even when there is no equality in the relationship. This closeness, this attachment, is almost limitless. Closeness in proximity isn't needed to feel and experience this bond.

When I am not near my partner, children, or guide, I still feel this strong connection. Of course, my physical contact with them is symbolized in a touch, kiss, or handshake. We literally make contact with our skin. I believe this touch is essential for me and for most of us. Through touch, I show my vulnerability, my compassion, and my good heart. Because it all starts with me. It's about going on a journey to find myself, getting to know myself, to feel real contact with myself. Then I can connect with others.

Coming home from my travels becomes coming home to myself.
And this is often scary and very challenging. It takes courage to look deeply into my actions and habits and their consequences. We all have patterns and habits from early childhood, which we carry with us. Our

family and environment create experiences we must live out, to heal certain wounds. It's most important we stay in touch with our true selves, while living and transforming our reactions and attitudes.

The journey is to stay connected to happiness and accept life's experiences. This boundless love for oneself is a superpower. It's our own inner guide, leading us to the people and situations we need to grow and evolve. When we accept our failings, strengths, desires, hopes, and doubts, we grow into ourselves and develop our personality. We might continue to attract the wrong people or actions. This is totally okay. As long as we are not hard on ourselves. As long as we allow ourselves to experiment and learn through doing. At a certain point, it is beneficial to start recognizing what is good for us and what isn't. It starts by looking more deeply into our actions, our habits, and their consequences. Because all actions have consequences.

By allowing ourselves to make the same mistake over and over because, at a certain point, so much experience and willpower are gained to transform it. This is such a transforming power. It allows happiness and pain to be embraced at the same time. As we go through life, we encounter so many experiences. Accept life with all its ups and downs. We always have something to learn.

If we recognize this in ourselves, then we might feel compassion for the other person. The other person is also learning, trying to embrace happiness and pain at the same time. We think the many things we experience, and especially the things that just happen to us, were done by the other person. We blame others for our faults and wrong doings. It's the world that has to change, not me!

On the journey of getting to know ourselves, many things come to the surface. Much of what we do is done unconsciously. When we learn more about ourselves, even hidden talents come to the surface. What a feast to discover!

It starts with recognizing our emotions, which are never created by the outside world, but through our inner world. There are four basic emotions: fear, happiness, anger, and sadness. All other emotions are derived from them. Anything triggering our emotions is worth exploring. It deepens our knowledge about ourselves, however confronting this might be. We don't want to feel shame or maybe anger in a group or with our family. But when we feel strong emotions towards a person or the outside world, it's usually due to our own pain and neglected feelings. In that moment, it's very difficult to see nuances.

Most often we have no idea what and why it happens. We get frustrated and irritated. Getting a handle on this is a very complex process. We need to start asking ourselves what the message is, what it has to teach us. We have to be brutally honest, endure difficult emotions and go through pain. Feeling this unbalance is courageous. In the end however, the reward is less stress, more energy, and happiness in our lives. Isn't that what we all want?

Introspection and guidance help us with finding ourselves and creating emotional balance. The superpower of love is the champion of all emotions. We need to nurture this compassion in ourselves, to find ourselves, to be free. But this is not enough. I am reminded of my ongoing journey. It's the trust in myself, the guidance of people around me, the difficult conversations, and the positive energy that continually leads me to my superpower of love.

To be really happy, we have to start recognizing our difficult emotions and where they turn up in our body. Traumas and fears are not only memories; they nestle in the body, like wounds. For example, when fearing to speak in public, muscles in the shoulders or back are the perfect place for fear to accumulate.

There are many ways to lighten up this fear and create energy, such as having a massage, practicing yoga, or Tai Chi. Emotional calmness starts with balancing our rich inner and outer world. And by seeing that an emotion like fear is not bad. It brings our inner world to our deeper self. By doing so, we recognize our worth. From this departure point, we are able to make our own, more supportive choices.

Certain emotional patterns, when triggered in adults or children, can set the stage for an entire drama played out within ourselves or between people. In our families, close relationships, and work environments, this kind of triggering can cause impulsive emotional reactions. None of these are mindful responses.

A Call to Action!

Energy flows where our attention goes. Cultivating your superpowers of self-esteem and self-compassion are ways to achieve emotional balance and boundless self-love. Develop habits that make you stronger. Start with allowing those emotions to be present. Cultivate a broader view, and with it, your potential. Let go of negative emotions in a mindful way, by finding stillness, going for a walk or maybe a meditation. Negative emotions are not bad. They are powerful signs for awakening and deeper healing. With these actions and habits, we transform our negative emotions.

You can't tailor the world to suit yourself, nor force it to fit into your vision of things. This doesn't mean you shouldn't aspire to make things better. The world is imperfect and likely to remain that way. No matter what situation you encounter, you can always strengthen your mind by incorporating it into your journey of getting to know yourself. This will lead you to ultimate happiness.

10

André Knol

***André Knol** is the founder and CEO of Innomics Enterprise Accelerator and co-founder of YesAndMore. André drives innovation, business, and social impact for small and medium-sized companies, large enterprises, and multinationals.*

His mission is creating a vehicle for innovation, transformation, and sustainable development in industries and regions in The Netherlands and abroad. Top-down, through innovation strategy facilitation and innovation portfolio management. And bottom-up, accelerating teams with a new mindset, skillset, and toolset, to compete in a world full of potential disruptions and social change. He is the author of several articles and books. Currently, André is writing a new book entitled 'Transformers Playbook – A guide for innovators and executives to build, develop, and scale the next wave of growth and sustainable progress'.

To Contact André: linkedin.com/in/andreknol
Founder and CEO, Innomics.nl | Co-founder YesAndMore/co

New Leadership to Help Solve the Global Challenges

Unforeseen financial and economic crises; excessive concentrations of wealth, power, and extreme wealth inequality; relentless resource depletion and pressure on the environment: our economy and society are in a deep systemic crisis.

People are increasingly radically insecure about their futures. The global crisis of society, economy, and supply chains (recently caused by COVID-19), shows us the fragility of the systems we have built. We need to develop our consciousness in businesses and institutional roles, or we might end up in conflicts, wars, and regression of our Sustainable Development Goals. On a world scale, we have never had so much money, resources, and technologies at our disposal which could serve the future of all. But the problem is, we are locked into the current systems, rules, and regulations, leading to an inability to change for good.

We need to transform our economy into a strong, open, trust-based, and vital system; to radically re-envision the system and unlock the present potential. We need to replace the dominant short-term, sectional, and self-regarding conception of our current economy. Our present economic and organizational principles help create fragmented and unilateral solutions, redundancy, and a critical loss in human and natural resources. The system is vulnerable, distrust based, fragile, and unsustainable.

We need to transform our economy into one which contributes to a future serving both the earth and our society. A balance shift is inevitable. Divisive and degenerative by default, it must be distributive and regenerative by design.

Women will lead the way

Over the past 20 years, I've had the opportunity and joy to drive innovation, business, and social impact for and with hundreds of large enterprises, multinationals, small and medium-sized companies, startups, and scale-ups. Only in the last five to ten years did I come to realize I could use this innovation and transformation mindset, skillset, and toolset for the societal challenges.

During my professional journey, I've read hundreds of management books on innovation, transformation, management, and leadership. Over the past 15 years, I have developed the crazy habit of making a top 50 list in my head at the end of a year of 'the best of the best people' in management and innovation. I've got hundreds of 'management and leadership heroes', the great thinkers and doers of modern economy and society.

Peter Drucker (1909 - 2005) is my absolute number 1 in this 'best-of' list. He has been described as 'the founder of modern management'. His writings contributed to the philosophical and practical foundations of the modern business corporation. He is closely followed by Rita Gunther McGrath, a strategic management scholar and professor of management at the Columbia Business School. She is regarded as one of the world's top experts on strategy, innovation, and entrepreneurship.

I confess, until recently, my top 50 list for these 15 years has been male dominated. Only 20% of this list consisted of female examples in management leadership in economics, business, and society. Rita Gunther McGrath was one of the few female examples making it to my top 10 every consecutive year.

I was never aware that my 'best-of' list was so male-dominated. The interesting thing is a major shift has taken place in my Top 50 list in recent years. Many women, with amazing new thinking and perspectives, have entered my top 50 list with high rankings. I asked myself, why?

This can be due to many things. Have I become more aware of women in leadership (hadn't I been paying attention all this time)? Has it been my personal development? Have more female examples, thinkers, and doers emerged? Is the zeitgeist different? Or is all the above combined or none of it the case?

And more importantly, why does this matter anyway? For me, that's the reason to contribute to this book. Because we must deepen feminine wisdom and leadership to face the global challenges and to shape the future that is needed in our world.

Who will run the world?

In my opinion, the world needs more feminine leadership, thinking and doing, now more than ever. Women like Kate Raworth, Mariana Mazzucato and Stephanie Kelton are the protagonists of this new movement, putting public purpose at the center of a circular economy.

Create to regenerate

"Economics is broken, and the planet is paying the price", as stated by Kate Raworth, author of the landmark book 'Doughnut Economics' (2017). For 200 years, industrial activities have been based on degenerative design. We take earth's materials, make them into stuff we want, use it for a while, and then toss it away. 'Take - Make - Use - Lose'. It's a one-way system, running counter to the living world. And it's devouring the resources of its own sustenance. Raworth is pushing for new visual maps and metaphors to represent sustainable growth that doesn't compromise future generations. What this means is moving away from the linear, upward moving line of 'progress' ingrained in us all, to a 'regenerative and distributive' model designed to engage everyone and shaped like a doughnut. The sweet spot is the dough of the doughnut; a system meeting all our needs without exhausting the planet. The safe and just space for humanity.

We must change to embed distributive regenerative design at the heart of our economies, if we choose to make it happen. And in all this, the 21st century economist's role is a crucial one: to harness the potential of business, finance, and human nature, to unleash this distributive regenerative future.

Mariana Mazzucato is a professor at University College London and the Founder/Director of the UCL Institute for Innovation and Public Purpose. Mazzucato is described as "one of the most forward-thinking economists of our times." In her seminal book 'The Entrepreneurial State' (2013) she invited us to rethink the role the state could have in the creation of wealth. This was followed by 'The Value of Everything: Making and Taking in the Global Economy' (2018), which demolished the widely held belief that a narrow economic elite was the wealth creator.

With her most recent book, 'Mission Economy' (2021), Mazzucato challenges governments to be more ambitious by ensuring the public good. A book that takes its cue from the Apollo 11 mission, it is full of vital ideas for progressives who want to change capitalism. This takes vision and strategy, two ingredients she says are too often sorely lacking. Especially post-COVID, purpose needs to be the driver determining the 'directionality' of focus, investments, and public/private partnerships. Governments should be using their power, both of investment and procurement, to orient efforts towards the big challenges on our horizon, not just the immediate short-term recovery.

Stephanie Kelton argues in her book 'The Deficit Myth' (2020), that we need strategic public investments in the future. Kelton offers us a brilliant exploration of modern monetary theory (MMT). This dramatically changes our understanding of how we can best deal with crucial issues ranging from poverty, inequality, job creation, expanding health care coverage, climate change, and building resilient infrastructure. Deficits can be used in good or bad ways but are themselves a neutral and powerful policy tool. "They can fund unjust wars that destabilize the world and cost millions their lives," she writes, "or they can be used to sustain life and build a more just economy that works for the many and not just the few." MMT gives us the power to imagine a new politics and a new economy, moving us from a narrative of scarcity to one of opportunity.

There are many more women, like Carlota Perez, Rebecca M. Henderson, Scilla Elworthy, and Jacinda Ardern, who are redefining economics and society all over the world.

Carlota Perez is currently Centennial Professor at the London School of Economics and, since 2006, Professor of Technology and Socio-Economic Development at Tallinn University of Technology, Tallinn, Estonia. The path-breaking book 'Technological Revolutions and Financial Capital' (2003) presents a novel interpretation of the good and bad times in the economy. It takes a long-term perspective and links technology and finance in an original and convincing way. It's the moment to shape the future for centuries to come.

Rebecca Henderson is a prominent economist, influential management and strategy professor at Harvard Business School and author of the new 'Reimagining Capitalism in a World on Fire' (2020), focused on driving large-scale change, providing solutions, and hope, for a world in crisis.

Scilla Elworthy has been nominated three times for the Nobel Peace Prize for her work with the Oxford Research Group to develop effective dialogue between nuclear weapons policy makers worldwide and their critics. She is the author of 'The Business Plan for Peace: Building a World Without War' (2017) and 'The Mighty Heart' (2020). Both publications offer the practical skills, knowledge and tried and tested strategies for preventing destructive conflict. If scaled-up and extended over 10 years, they can prevent armed violence worldwide and enable leaders to make wiser decisions, so that there is less suffering as a result of war.

And finally, Jacinda Ardern, the 40th prime minister of New Zealand and leader of the Labor Party since 2017, is another game changer. Ardern's administration has focused particularly on the New Zealand housing crisis, child poverty and social inequality. In March 2019, she led the country through the aftermath of the Christchurch mosques shootings, rapidly introducing strict gun laws in response. Throughout 2020, she directed the country's response to the COVID-19 pandemic, which has been praised and endorsed worldwide.

The watchwords of the aforementioned powerhouse women are all about challenging the orthodoxy of growth, changing capitalism and balancing economic sustainability with the need for social and ecological sustainability.

Deepening feminine wisdom

The balance shift we urgently need to make is an extremely difficult one. But the problem is, we are locked into current systems rules which lead to an inability to change for good. The way we are conditioned, our organizations, management, and processes are insufficiently geared to solve this.

"To shape the future that is needed in our world, we must bring the feminine back into balance with the masculine. Feminine wisdom has been marginalized for centuries and is desperately needed to address the challenges we now face," as Scilla Elworthy puts it very clearly.

Making the shift from a predominantly masculine 'command and control' style of leadership to a more feminine, collaborative style of meta-leadership is hard and requires a completely different skill set. Many senior leaders in large corporate environments completed their education in the universities and MBA schools of the 'achievement' era, characterized by the machine-type organization. They are used to coming up with the answers and telling people what they need to do. It's how they've always been rewarded and how they got to where they are today!

In the past two or three decades, however, we've begun to experience increasing levels of complexity and uncertainty, impacting almost every aspect of our lives. We are traversing this 'change of eras', characterized by rapid change, accelerating technological and scientific breakthroughs, with an unprecedented level of competitiveness. Perhaps the biggest hurdle to making this shift in leadership style involves learning to 'let go'. This encompasses getting comfortable with ambiguity and uncertainty, while appreciating diversity of thinking and listening to ideas. It also comprises of finding common ground and involving others in decision making; something many senior level corporate leaders today find extremely uncomfortable, especially when they're required to admit they don't have all the answers.

We must change the rules to bring business back into balance with the planet. It is possible to create a better, more sustainable future. "It seems that our key challenge is how to shift from an economic system based on the notion of unlimited growth to one that is both ecologically sustainable and socially just. 'No growth' is not the answer. Growth is a central characteristic of all life; a society, or economy, that does not grow will die sooner or later. Growth in nature, however, is not linear and unlimited. While certain parts of organisms, or ecosystems grow, others decline, releasing and recycling their components which become resources for new growth," as stated by Fritjof Capra and Hazel Henderson in their book 'Qualitative Growth (2013).

Transitioning to an integral regenerative logic implies that economies and societies are embedded parts of the biosphere. We need to restore, renew, or revitalize our own and shared sources of energy and materials to create resilient and equitable systems that integrate the needs of society with the integrity of nature.

All over the world, in all systems, we see the devastation caused by the old ways of thinking that cut across societies, geographies and generations. Feminine Intelligence, available to men as it is to women, is needed to face the current crises and bring a radical shift in the way we live and lead.

A Call to Action!

Share this essay with all the men you know in leadership positions. Let them know that developing their female intelligence is not a sign of weakness but actually a sign of strength.

For all the female leaders reading this essay, don't suppress your feminine intelligence. Let it shine through in all you do and say.

11

Wendy Broersen

Wendy Broersen *is a serial entrepreneur, international speaker, founder, and CEO of the international company Superwomen/Superpeople Academy, and curious as hell. Superpeople Academy helps companies to attract, retain, and develop a diverse workforce. We do things in unconventional ways when we see things aren't moving fast enough or in the right direction. We offer executive coaching, D&I consultancy, and training in VR for unconscious bias awareness.*

Wendy developed Equalitypoly, which is the first management diversity game to successfully help companies to not just talk about diversity and inclusion but get into action, to do something. In addition, her Ambition Program for talented women has won an award.

→ *To contact Wendy: linkedin.com/in/wendybroersen*
superwomenacademy.com

Why You Need Men in Your Life to Be Successful

Before you send me hate mail, I am a feminist at heart. I will explain in this essay why I believe you need men in your life. I will also give you tips on how to increase the percentage of men in your network. And I will provide you with some tips on how to be a male ally, which you can give to the men in your life.

Men have the power

The fact is most of the power still lies with men. I wish this were not the case, but it is reality. It is changing towards a more balanced situation, which in my opinion, should be 50-50 but we aren't there yet. The best way to achieve this balance is to make sure you get some of the power. And give some of that power to other women.

So, what's a woman to do?

And yes, get used to the word woman because any woman over 18 should not be called a girl anymore. It makes people think of them differently. Don't you think it's strange most people don't use the word boy anymore when they grow older, yet the word girl is still there in the workplace? I am drifting away from the topic, but take heed of my words, please.

The most shocking facts of all

In general, more than 30% of the women in the world are not financially independent. And, whether we like it or not, money is power. So, if you are one of those women, you make decisions that are partly driven by your dependence on income. Sadly, I know many women who have gotten into financial difficulties when they got divorced or widowed. In some cases, they even decided to stay with their husband because of their financial dependence.

You can't ask men to fix that, but you can take steps towards that financial independence. Here are some suggestions and tips:

- If you have children, don't take that step back in hours but take on that responsibility together. For instance, a good step is to both work one day less.
- Another good example is to go to a retirement expert and do the numbers, taking into account if your partner dies before you.
- Make sure you divide household tasks evenly, including taking care of the elderly (parents).
- Make sure you receive equal pay. One of the reasons why women earn less is because the unequal payment starts at their first job. Men, in general, ask for higher wages and more extras. And the financial impact of those extras can be significant, especially when you add them up over the years. Since most of the management is still male (on average 66%), you need men in your corner to change this.
- Dare to ask; the worst thing that can happen to you, is when they say no. But if you don't ask you already have a no. Women are great negotiators for others, but when it comes to negotiating for themselves, they drop the ball. No worries, take a course in negotiating, which pays itself back in no time (every month when you look at your paycheck!).

Politics

The fact is men dominate the majority of governments. And to create legislation that evens out the playing field for women, we need those men on our side. I dare to say that if men would menstruate, did most of the caretaking of children, and gave birth, a lot of those rules and laws would be in place already. Inequality is often not intentional. It's simply because they do not experience the consequences of the inequality. New drugs should be tested on 50-50 F/M groups, getting rid of 'period poverty', paid leave for men who just become parents, and a quota on boards for companies, are only a few examples which can make a significant change in the position of women.

So, we need the men in those positions to care about all of that. Of course, it would be even better if more women would be in office. And for that to happen, women need to vote more often for women, and more men should vote for women.

No need to be negative

I did not write this article to be negative or pessimistic. There's enough of that in the world already. The fact of the matter is, most men would gladly welcome being more involved in taking care of their children, having more female colleagues, not being the primary breadwinner, and living in a world offering equal opportunities to both men and women. But they often don't know how to help or where to start. So, here are a few things men can do. And you can give them a little nudge in that direction.

Fathers

Make a list of all the tasks in your household, great and small, which need to be done every day/week/month/year. And then divide them evenly. Start the conversation about taking care of children (even before having them). Knowing or not knowing how to do those tasks, personal likes/dislikes can be taken into account but should not be reasons not to have them on your list. Why else do we have YouTube? Everything can be figured out with a bit of help from your friends at Google and YouTube.

Managers

Women are different. And that's good, because diversity brings better decisions, more innovations, and happier employees. But they are different. To evaluate them in the same way, by male standards, is not working well for women. As a leader, it is your responsibility to make sure all your team members can thrive. The easiest way is to make all evaluation processes inclusive is with more facts, and less personal (subjective) evaluations. If you do want to include personal assessments, make sure more than one person does this, to counter possible unconscious biases.

Male Mentors / Male Sponsors

The importance and value of having a mentor, I need not explain. But if you are working in a male-dominated industry, having a male mentor can be of extra value. In Dutch, we have a proverb: "je moet weten hoe de hazen lopen", which roughly translated into "you have to know how the hares run". It speaks to the importance of knowing how people behave to be successful. Just like hunters need to know, so they have better aim, that hares, when they flee, run in a zig-zag pattern.

It would be even better if you get yourself a male sponsor. Ideally, that is someone who is 2 tiers above you in the hierarchy and has already expressed that he sees great potential in you. A sponsor is someone who actively promotes you and helps you to take the next step in your career. He will bring you to important meetings, let you present, and gives you tasks that will put you in the spotlight. In short, all actions are aimed to get you on the shortlist for that next promotion. And, most importantly, he does this openly.

And, when you have that mentor or sponsor, do the same for another woman!

Balance your network

Most women know a lot of men, most men know a lot of other men. Since most of the power is thus with men, it is time to broaden your network by actively connecting with men. Of course, it is more difficult with us working from home, but I will give you a couple of examples which work anywhere in the world, any time. And remember, you build this network to benefit from it in the future.

First, when in a video conference, make time to connect before or after on LinkedIn with all the men in that meeting. Preferably the ones with a higher position, for whom you are not a threat.

Second, schedule (virtual) coffee dates. Find a man who is one or two tiers up, give him a compliment and schedule a coffee date to talk about his career and how he did it. You always learn from stories like that and, if you play your cards right, you gain a male ally to help you with your ambitions.

Third, look beyond your organization and connect with male clients, suppliers, and partners of your organization. They, like you, will not stay forever in their organization and/or in the position they are in now. They can also recommend you because you are not a threat to them.

A Call to Action!

After reading all this, I hope you realize now I don't want women to depend on the men in their lives. I think we need men in women's lives to create change faster and easier. And I genuinely believe we, men and women, will be happier in an equal world with all the benefits diversity brings.

I've given you enough tips in this essay, so enough talking; let's get into action!

12 Tessa van Keeken

Tessa van Keeken *specializes in building bridges and holding space, so everyone can feel seen, heard, and loved. She believes in empowering people to shine authentically and cultivate meaningful relationships, with themselves and others.*

She is an experienced coach and healer, with a background in Social Science and International Relations & Conflict Studies. Tessa guides conscious leaders and change makers on a transformational journey of self-discovery including personal, professional, and spiritual growth. She helps people to (re)connect to their inner wisdom and rise to life's challenges, so they can feel more balanced to live and lead with authentic presence.

Tessa is the founder of the Embrace movement, bringing those supporting others together, which she considers paramount for making the world a better place. The global community offers a safe space to tend to your own healing and growth. This is essential to practice inner leadership and serve others best.

Having lived in Ireland for 15 years, Tessa now resides in her home country, The Netherlands.

→ *To contact Tessa: linkedin.com/in/tessavankeeken*
tessavankeeken.com

Living and Leading with Authentic Presence: Embrace Your True Self

"Waking up to who you are requires letting go of who you imagine yourself to be." Alan Watts

How many times have you described yourself by listing the things you do, have done in the past, or plan to do in the future? Telling people about your 'roles': parent, partner, employee or employer, professional or entrepreneur, introvert or extrovert?

But is that who you really are? What if your role changed from being a partner to being an ex? Or from employed to unemployed? Would you then no longer be yourself? Of course, when changes happen in life, sometimes we don't feel like ourselves. But is that because we really aren't or because it takes time to adjust, especially if our sense of self is attached to something we can't (fully) control, such as being a partner or employed?

Paradoxically, to truly be ourselves, we need to let go of holding on to the identity we create. Your true self is not your own imagined ideal, a perfect edition of Ms. or Mr. [your name].

When you embark on a journey of self-discovery to become your true self, you probably ask yourself: 'who am I'?

But the real question you need to ask yourself is: 'where am I'?

Getting lost in the search of finding yourself

Many of the people I work with feel lost. Yet, I don't help people find themselves. Rather, I empower them to embrace their true self. One of my clients put it into words perfectly at the end of her coaching journey with me: "I thought I was lost and needed to find myself. But I realized I do not have to get to know myself. I know myself already. I have to (learn to) accept myself, through understanding."

You can only understand and accept who you truly are when you are present. Who you truly are is all of you: everything you've been, everything you are, and everything you will become. You can learn from your past and plan for your future, but you can only BE here, now. Since you are constantly changing and growing, you cannot fully know who you will become.

As long as you keep searching for yourself, you will stay lost. Especially when you are searching outside yourself. Yet, to be present, with and within yourself, it's not enough to be aware of your own view of yourself. You also need to be aware of how others relate to you, how you are being perceived.

You are you in relation to

Often, people think being yourself is just about themselves. 'Here I am. Take it or leave it, I don't care what you think of me'. This may sound self-confident, but it often overshadows a lack of self-belief and self-acceptance.

If you don't care what others think, or how they perceive you, you create a disconnect between you and the outside world. You do not exist in isolation. You are you in relation to: to yourself, others, and the world.

If you lack awareness of how you are being perceived, you may still feel lost and only find yourself when you pay attention to this. This can happen quite literally.

In Iceland, a search and rescue was set in motion when a tourist failed to return to the tour bus after a stop at a canyon. Only many hours later, the search was called off when a woman, who was herself taking part in the search, realized it was her they were looking for. It turned out the driver miscounted and the passengers did not recognize the woman, as she had changed clothes. And the woman in question did not realize they were talking about her, as, in turn, she did not recognize herself in the description of her.

Even if you feel people aren't seeing you as you truly are, only when you are open to listen to how they perceive you, can you learn how you being you is expressed and experienced in the world. The world you are part of.

I prefer to say: 'I deeply care what you think of me but I'm not dependent on it'. This is, of course, only true when I am in a state of self-acceptance. Otherwise, I actually do feel dependent on what others think of me. Besides making sure you stay open to how others perceive you, this way of being allows you to check in with yourself to determine if you are accepting yourself.

Awareness and being truly honest with yourself

Another misconception is the idea that accepting, embracing, and being your true self means you should always do what you want, regardless of the circumstances. Again, this happens when there is a disconnect from being yourself in relation to others. As you are not living in isolation, your expression of your true self can be flexible. It doesn't mean you can never do or say things that are not fully aligned with who you are.

Authenticity, being your true self, isn't necessarily about what you do or say, but much more about *why* you do it. It's not about your reasoning but about your true intention.
Let me illustrate this:
It was my father's birthday. He values etiquette, especially when going out for dinner. I don't really care for chic clothes, but it means a lot to

him. I decided to wear clothes my father likes. Was this an act of being or denying my true self? That depends on my underlying thoughts and feelings, my intention:

- 'I'll wear clothes my father likes to make him happy, otherwise he may get annoyed. I don't want to feel rejected.' (denying my true self).
- 'I'll wear clothes my father likes to make him happy, because he will appreciate it. I want him to feel comfortable. It feels good doing this.' (being my true self).

Similarly, if I had decided not to wear clothes my father likes, it depends on the why, whether this was being my true self. The key is to be aware whether your decisions and actions are coming from a grounded space of compassion, for yourself and others, or whether they are infused by fear.

Here's what often happens though: if you feel it's wrong to do something out of fear, you may tell yourself you're doing it out of caring. If you feel the need to rigidly uphold your identity, this is often a sign you're not fully accepting yourself as you are. For instance, if I decided to wear the clothes I prefer out of fear of not being me, it is questionable whether this could be considered being my true self.

Be honest with yourself.

You are not your values: your true self isn't set in stone

"He who defines himself can't know who he really is." Lao Tzu (Tao Te Ching)

If it doesn't really matter what you do, then how do you truly express being your true self? Some people believe it's all about living in alignment with your core values. However, it's important to understand that although your core values guide you to stay true to who you are and to act in alignment with what matters to you, it's not the values themselves that determine your true self.

Let's explore this. Have you ever done an exercise to determine your core values? Where you figure out which 3-5 values resonate with you the most, that make you feel fulfilled and aligned.

Now, I would like to invite you to go back to a time when you were in a different phase of your life. Do you recognize that some of the values you consider to be core values now, probably weren't at that age, or the other way around?

For instance, someone may have considered 'adventure' an absolute must in their 20s, but in their 40s 'stability' has become essential for them to feel in flow. Also, many people in their 30's, 40's and 50's list 'family' as a core value, yet this might not have been true in their teens.

This is where we see how we can only be our true self in this moment, in the present. We can't know now whether a core value will always remain core, or whether it will shift over time. It's pointless to try and find out. It takes our presence away from where we are now and therefore, away from our true selves. Remember, values, even core ones, are fundamental beliefs. They are fundamental but they are beliefs, nonetheless.

When supporting clients struggling to determine what is truly important for them, I often ask: 'What are your true deal breakers regarding this issue? What absolutely needs to be a certain way for you to feel ok?' If they are considering a new career or role, an answer might be: 'I only want to work in a small organization, because I value feeling connected and I don't want to be a pawn in an anonymous corporate company.'

I then ask: 'So, what if...', mentioning a scenario where the situation would be exactly as they described, except for this one thing they stated is a deal breaker, 'could you think of any reason why you would still be ok with it? Truly ok.'
You know what the most common response is? 'It depends...', followed by something it depends on.

The truth is, hardly anything, if anything at all, is completely set in stone within yourself, that doesn't depend on your relationship to the world around you in that moment.

Looking back at your life, have you ever ended up in a job, relationship, or situation, that in the past you would have sworn wasn't aligned with your values or being true to yourself, but which turned out to be exactly what you needed and actually made you feel in flow? Which, in fact, allowed you to be your true self?

The key to being your true self: Acceptance in this moment

If you can't find your true self, if you can't define or shape it, how can you be your true self and know you are true to yourself? It all circles back to accepting yourself as you are, in this moment. Acceptance and awareness are key to take aligned actions. To be able to accept yourself, you need to be fully aware; aware of when you are in flow in the moment, aware of how you relate to others and the world.

Be mindful of the danger of the desire to move straight into action when you become aware of what is present for you in this moment. Especially if you don't like it. If you can't accept it, you might try to hide these parts, thus stopping yourself from being your true self.

If you move into action without acceptance, ultimately, everything becomes a struggle. A constant upholding of the image or ideal of yourself, which you would like others to see as your true self, leads to feeling disconnected, as you never truly feel in your flow.

Accepting yourself isn't an act of complacency, of stopping your development and growth; of thinking 'ah well, this is just the way I am'. It simply means you can accept yourself as you are, in *this* moment in time. To embrace both your light and your shadows *in this moment*, and to take aligned action from this place. Practicing acceptance allows you to stay fully open to what may come onto your path and gives you the best chance of succeeding in being your true self.

A Call to Action!

How does this relate to female leadership? Self-development has become more widely accepted among both women and men. However, anything to do with deep inner exploration and being in touch with your true self is often still seen as feminine. Especially in more corporate settings. It's something seen as reserved for people in caring professions. The rise of female leadership is crucial for making this more the norm in all areas of work and society.

Each moment you are truly present here and now, with full acceptance of yourself and what is, you allow yourself to be your true self and the ancestor of your future true self. Contributing to a more authentic world.

So, ask yourself: '*where* am I, now?'

13

Rosemary Amato

Rosemary Amato *is a CMA, CISA, CPA (Inactive) and a Six-Sigma Green belt. Rosemary is a modern day example of someone who is never afraid to challenge the status quo while relishing everything the world has to offer even when unexpected change occurs. And change has occurred many times for Rosemary.*

As an American with a career spanning the US, The Netherlands, and Malta, she successfully moved through the ranks in finance and IT in the manufacturing, retail, and distribution industries. Rosemary then made the big change of moving to Deloitte, where she spent over 20 years serving clients in over 20 countries. She was also privileged to serve on the Global boards of IMA and ISACA, and now sits on the peer review team for the AACSB. She is the owner of Romarat Consultancy.

→ *To contact Rosemary: linkedin.com/in/rosemaryamato*

Facts – Memories – Plans: Just Data!

I remember the first time a boss said to me: "Rosemary, you have to broaden your grey area. Everything is not black or white. The sooner you figure that out, the sooner you will be a success." Broaden my grey area? What did he mean? I'll come back to that shortly, as that sentence really summarizes the need for every individual to be data intelligent. And I want to share with you how I discovered data intelligence.

Ever since I was a child, I focused on getting the facts. I learned that when you present the facts, people will listen to you. I have always been an avid reader, starting with the summer reading program at Harvey Rice School in Cleveland, Ohio, USA. I also learned that facts make you start thinking that everything is black and white, wrong or right, left or right, and so forth. And that attitude stayed with me while I was growing up in my blue-collar family.

My parents were second generation immigrants. Dad's parents came from Sicily and my mother's parents came from Hungary. They were focused on having their three daughters go to college. The facts presented to my sisters and myself were that we would go to a college prep high school and there would be no discussion over this fact. The school they chose for us, after researching a lot of data, was a school that prided itself on making students ready for college. And yes, all three of us were accepted at the same high school and then we were accepted into the colleges we each chose. I became an accountant, and my sisters became medical doctors.

Looking back at my memories from my early career days, I wonder why I made the choices I did. I realize now that I often didn't have enough data when I decided to move from employer to employer, from city to city, from country to country. From the age of 21 to 47, I had 7 employers and 10 different roles. I moved between states 7 times. My motivation for taking a new role or moving to a new company was purely money. I wasn't gathering all the data I needed to make a decision; I was just gathering facts. Only one of those facts was a real data field: how much money would the new role/position pay? I've since realized that I made some good decisions with the moves, but I also made some bad ones.

I learned that most people, including myself at that time in my life, don't think about gathering data in order to make a good decision. They just want to decide. I know I gathered a variety of facts. I created action plans from those facts, but was it really data? And was it the data I needed to make an informed decision? And most importantly, was it good data? We know the world is rapidly changing and evolving into a world where fake news appears regularly. How do you know if your data is good? How do you recognize what data you need? How do you plan for your future with data? I'm still struggling with data and there is no simple answer.

During my career, after the age of 47 until I was forced to retire at the age of 66 (and that is another story!), I worked for one company, in one location. I served clients, working on various projects in cities throughout the world. Data was always the focus for these projects: auditing data, data in E-Business, risks of using data, Big Data, data to validate computer systems, data visualizations. Almost every project was focused on data and how it was created, retained, changed, or used. But one thing that was often missing from the project was the answer to the question: *WHY?*

Why were those clients concerned about data? What questions were they trying to answer? Why was the data needed? Would they change something? Would something improve? The WHY is the most important aspect of understanding data, but everyone forgets to ask that question.

I remember a seminar I attended in London when Big Data was the new buzz word. One of the speakers was an ex-employee from Barclays Bank. That is where I learned about the importance of WHY. He showed example after example of initiatives that failed and initiatives that succeeded. The key to a successful initiative was that someone asked the question *WHY* and had hypotheses prepared to answer that question. *WHY* do we need to collect this data? *WHY* is this data important to us? And then, what are we going to do after we analyze the data?

Today, we are still being bombarded with data. How many surveys do you receive a week? Survey after survey; someone is collecting data for some reason. Newspapers, whether online or those still in print, have sections with charts, even on non-financial topics. They are trying to use data to prove a point they want to make. I have learned that you can prove anything by preparing a good data visualization; but does it always tell the truth? Only you can judge that, by learning how to read a visualization. *WHY* is this visualization being presented to you? Do they want you to vote for someone? Do they want you to buy a product? Do they want you to invest in some money offering or stock? You must become data intelligent. Understand how data is being collected and why it is being channeled to the audience it is focused on. Nothing may be further from the truth than a visualization that appears to use the facts. If you don't know how to interpret it and you don't have an understanding of what data they used to prepare it, you can be taken advantage of.

This is the challenge we all have now. Remember what my boss said to me: broadening my grey area? I learned that all decisions I made, and will still have to make, are not black and white. There are very few things that fall into a black or white category. Broadening my grey area has allowed me to look at facts, compare data, and realize that most situations fall into the grey area. Those things that are not life or death. Those things that I can accept a compromise for. The author of

'The Da Vinci Code', Dan Brown said: "I love the grey area between right and wrong. It is here where the actions of conflict or cooperation take place. It is here that our world of emotion can be uncovered. The grey areas of life allow us to choose sides and form our alliances. It is here where we can become enemies of our opposers. So much of human interaction is lived in the grey areas."

And living in the grey areas means you have to ask the question *WHY*.

A Call to Action!

This is the message I have for you today. Become data intelligent by understanding your need for data in your life, and not just in your business life. Get the facts, do the research, and broaden your grey area. While broadening your grey area, always ask the question *WHY*. Why am I concerned about this? Why should I dig deeper into the data?

As I started to recognize that very few things are black and white, I learned to broaden my grey area. More opportunities opened up for me, especially when I asked the question *WHY*. I also used data to close doors when necessary and I did stick to the black or white when I absolutely felt there was no grey area. I'm sure you, too, will recognize the importance of being data intelligent. Learn how to broaden your grey area by focusing on the facts. Do the research, get good data, and then create your plans and make decisions as a data intelligent individual. Incorporate data into your life! And always remember to ask Why!

14

Nico Samaras

Nico Samaras *is a third culture kid who has travelled and lived in several countries. He has made the Netherlands home but also remains loyal to his wonderful homeland, Greece. He kicked off his early career working for the family in traditional Greek fashion, until he went to the Netherlands.*

Nico entered the corporate world and very quickly rose to the top in sales & marketing, closing major contracts across EMEA and the Americas. Drawing on his entrepreneurial background, corporate achievements, and personal goals, he is now doing what he loves most: as CEO of his brand ETIMY.COM he supports High Performing executives on their way to becoming their 'best selves'.

- *Goals and aspirations: To help decision makers become more empathetic and compassionate, without compromising corporate culture and profitability*
- *Most notable achievement: Supporting coaches with their clients who are mostly highly successful executives across EMEA.*

To contact Nico: linkedin.com/in/nico-samaras-mba
ETIMY.COM

Become Your Best Self

My personal motivation for writing this essay is to provide a real-life story to support your leadership journey, to become your 'Best Self'. First and foremost, for the people you love most, for those you lead and ultimately, for yourself.

My mother lost her father at nine years of age. She was a widow at 24, with two children tagging along. My father was tragically taken from us at the age of 30, in a construction accident caused by corporate negligence. My father didn't come home to his family that evening. He didn't turn up for myself, my sister, and my mother ever again. An empty seat stood where he previously sat.

Like many women in similar circumstances, my mother, now a widow, had to endure and succeed in a male dominated society of yesteryear. It was a world far more cruel to single women and by far, more unforgiving than today, often with no laws to protect her and her children.

Resolute in her determination

My mother never relented. She was a strong-minded woman who stopped at nothing to protect us, but also achieved what she wanted. She accomplished this whilst dedicating her life to her children. By the age of 30, she ran several corporations (with her future husband), including butcheries and a casino. I grew up in that household and saw this young woman I called 'Mom', work five days a week, 8 am to 5 pm. Each Wednesday and Saturday, she went to work again at the casino, from 8 pm to 4 am. She never got burnt out or depressed. She loved what she did but also knew there was no other option. She was resolute and determined to be a successful female professional, for our sake. Her motivation was fueled by a powerful reason to succeed: her children.

Ready for what life brings

I started my Coaching Platform, ETIMY.COM, which is a Greek word (έτοιμη) meaning 'readiness' or 'completely prepared', where we help professionals overcome barriers to achieve their goals and ambitions. The initial concept was derived from my upbringing, watching my mother achieve so much in a male dominated society, while being both mother and father to her children. No one is completely prepared for what life might bring, but what you do in those circumstances makes or breaks you. I believe that if you aren't 'ready', no amount of learning, education, coaching, or consultation will help you succeed. This became my aim: to help individuals remove barriers for the betterment of their own personal leadership and become 'ready' ETIMY (έτοιμη) for what's to come.

Leadership versus Management[1]

In the chart below, you can see the fundamental differences between leaders and managers:

Business Manager	Vs	Business Leader
Managers Administer		Leaders Innovate
Managers Maintain		Leaders Develop
Managers Control		Leaders Inspire
Managers Have A Short Term View		Leaders Ask What And Why
Managers Imitate		Leaders Originate
Managers Accept the Status Quo		Leaders Challenge It

Building a team of leaders better than yourself

It's misleading to think that good leadership is just common sense. True leadership is when you are constantly looking to replace yourself by someone better than yourself. Simultaneously, you are as strong as the people you surround yourself with. Richard Hughes[1], a guru on leadership, speaks about 'exemplary followers' who present a consistent picture to both leaders and co-workers: being independent, innovative and willing to stand up to superiors. They are also your eyes and ears. When you are an Interactive leader, your followers are excited about what they are doing and feel appreciated. You exemplify a significant female leadership trait towards getting the best out of your people who then, in turn, create your own greatness.

Most successful companies attract highly capable workforces, educated with the ability to think for the client without executive interference. In fact, sometimes it's better to have a sleeping CEO, than a meddling CEO.

Networking gets you the position

One of the quickest ways to get promoted is by networking. Stephen P. Robbins[2] speaks of average, successful and effective managers. Highly successful managers spend 48% of their time networking, yet effective managers spend 44% communicating. Note that 'successful' managers are defined in terms of the speed of promotion within their organization.

The power of empathy and compassion

A Forbes article entitled 'The Psychopathic CEO' states: "Roughly 4% to as high as 12% of CEOs exhibit psychopathic traits, according to some expert estimates, many times more than the 1% rate found in the general population and more in line with the 15% rate found in prisons."[3] That's scary by any standards!

Being compassionate is not the same as being empathetic. While empathy refers more generally to our ability to take the perspective and feel the emotions of another person, compassion is when those feelings and thoughts include the desire to help[4]. It is your responsibility as a business leader to help others. You have the obligation, responsibility, and biological makeup to be a compassionate business leader, not a manager.

It's challenging enough for male professionals to succeed in the matrixed corporate ladder; how much more so for a female professional trying to enter the male dominated, often gender discriminated environments? Luckily, since 2006, the Norwegian government set a precedence and "introduced quota legislation that required both public and state-owned companies to have 40% female board representation by 2008."[5] This is a significant step, in my opinion, towards normalization, transparency and accountability. I have often said the executive team spends most of its effort just getting to that position. Once they achieve the 'hot seat', they often forget the real reason that inspired them to reach the top (to help people) and go on an experimentation rampage without taking responsibility for their (often 'negative') actions.

Self-compassionate mindfulness

In her book, Kristin Neff, who is the founder of Self-compassionate Mindfulness, speaks about being kind to yourself. It's a powerful way to heal destructive emotional patterns, be healthier and happier in parenting, or other trials we face on a daily basis. What is even more intriguing is that in her 'Loving-Kindness Meditation'[6], she calls upon the participant to think of someone who has been 'unconditionally kind to you'. She asks that you give love and goodwill to that person, and then cross-transfer those same emotions to be compassionate to yourself. It's much easier to be kind to someone else, rather than use that compassion on yourself. It's not enough to be compassionate or empathetic to others; you need to be compassionate to yourself as well.

An extreme example that changed my leadership forever

In the article on Organizational Behavior[7], SP Robbins explains how a successful US female executive was faced with rampant theft at her company's plant in China. Through her perseverance and determination, she managed to catch one of the elusive thieves. He had attempted to steal something small, possibly to sell it and feed his family. The manager dutifully handed him over to the police and as you'd have it, he was summarily executed!

That small paragraph changed my whole perception about the people I lead. I hope this tragic event has a lasting effect on all who read it. This short article touches on each aspect of the minimum required by us to lead fellow human beings. Impeccable leadership requires us to avert tragedy; through understanding culture shock, personal leadership, empathy, compassion, and the ability to judge fairly. Above all else, to listen intently to our subordinates and ask 'why?'. Indeed, this is an extreme example of leadership but it's a true reminder of the consequences of our decisions which, once set in motion, cannot be undone.

A Call to Action!

The world is out there, waiting for you, needing you to succeed. There are more opportunities and support for female professionals now than in any other period in the history of mankind.

Each step you take towards achieving your goals and ambitions as a female leader, know that another woman has made it to the top before you, and many more will make if after you. Often times with far less support than you have had. Take the steps you need: the mentoring, the coaching, the networking, and sponsoring to become your 'Best Self'.

Footnotes

1 Richard Hughes et Al (2012)Leadership: Enhancing the Lessons of Experience, McGraw-Hill/Irwin
2 Robbins S.P. (2005) Organizational Behavior, New Jersey, Prentice Hall
3 Jack McCollough, Forbes: https://www.forbes.com/sites/jackmccullough/2019/12/09/the-psychopathic-ceo/
4 https://greatergood.berkeley.edu/topic/compassion/definition
5 Wikipedia:https://en.wikipedia.org/wiki/Gender_representation_on_corporate_boards_ of_directors#Europe
6 Kristine Neff 2015 Self-Compassion: The Proven Power of Being Kind to Yourself, by Dr. Kristin Neff
7 Robbins S.P. (2005) Organizational Behavior, New Jersey, Prentice Hall

15

Blanca Vergara

***Blanca Vergara** is a miracle whisperer, alchemist, MBA, and real life Aztec shaman. She is a modern spiritual business mentor. Blanca's work integrates the wisdom of ancestral traditions with contemporary science and business. She helps female entrepreneurs transform ancestral mental blocks into profound wisdom, happiness, and wealth.*

Her childhood trauma gives her an authentic and profound understanding of what it takes for healing and thriving to take place, especially for women.

She is a soul and business mentor for international female business owners and helps them transmute their Female Lineage into their unlimited source of power. After working with her, they succeed and bloom on every level.

Blanca is the author of several books, including among others, 'Unstoppable You' and 'Women Work Wonders'. She lives in Amsterdam with her two children and her husband. She also speaks Spanish and Dutch.

→ *To contact Blanca: linkedin.com/in/blancavergara*
blancavergara.com

Wounds, Wealth, and Wisdom

What do you feel when you read the following facts?

- Less than 6% of Fortune 500 companies have female CEO's.[1]
- American women are 80% more likely to be in poverty after retirement than men.[2]
- 61% of women said they would rather talk about death than money.[3]
- Only 24% of federal politicians worldwide are women.[4]

Are you angry when you see these numbers? At the system, men, your mother, your father, the patriarchy? You've done all the business trainings. You work so hard. Yet the big bucks and happiness appear to be a fiction of your imagination. You feel you should have had it all together by now, yet it's still not happening for you.

Helpless?

Do you feel this is an impossible battle? That you'll never be able to be 'one of them': a successful and happy woman?

Being emotionally triggered by these facts is precisely what keeps women away from having massive impact and financial success. This emotional response, whether blame, shame, or guilt, is triggered by an invisible 'enemy' created by the consciousness of the past 12,000 years.

For the last 12 millenniums, we developed a consciousness of separation: good and bad, left and right, above and below, spirit and matter, rich and poor, holy and evil. While the masculine has been celebrated, the feminine has been vilified, repressed, or plainly forgotten by most cultures. This consciousness of separation is at the core of the human experience in the past centuries: wars, poverty, pollution, gender inequalities and much more. This has affected every single living being on this planet.

This divisive consciousness created a deeply engrained inner enemy in all women: the Ancestral Female Trauma. This is a set of the non-supportive beliefs that keeps us women invisible and financially weak.

What is the Ancestral Female Trauma (AFT)

My own money story exemplifies it very well. The first life chapter was all about being a success in the masculine way. I was a successful executive: the poster perfect girl of 'Woman to the Top'. I was the 'man' for the job. My life was dominated by the rejection of the feminine and the desire to be accepted as 'good' by 'them' (the system, men, my mother, my father, the patriarchy)

The AFT sounded in my head as:

- Hard work is the only path to attainment
- Giving the answer they expect is the only way towards success
- Saying yes will bring me great financial rewards and relationships

At some point my body and soul were tremendously hungry for the feminine. I had my period twice a year. Symptoms of an imminent heart attack and burnout were not rare. So, I quit my corporate career and dove into everything spiritual and emotional. It was a great choice, as it allowed love and motherhood to enter my life.

Yet, my wallet wasn't very pleased. I became financially dependent on my husband. No matter how hard I worked and how much I learned, the very last second before success, I would sabotage myself for no apparent reason. In this chapter of my life, the AFT also ran my life. Now it sounded like:

- If I make money, my husband will leave me
- I cannot earn more than my husband
- If I make more money, they'll take it away from me
- If I make money, they'll think I'm a bad person

It was not until I took out my very own skeleton in the closet, my own Ancestral Female Trauma, that my business started growing. I noticed that whenever I avoided it, I would easily go back to self-sabotaging thoughts and actions. However, when I dared to look it in the eye and see it for what it is, a series of painful lies keeping women small and humanity in separation, then magic would happen.

- Without additional action, I got more customers
- I could name my price with ease and sell without feeling dirty
- I found short cuts to ease my work

What feeds the Ancestral Female Trauma?

There are two main reinforcing mechanisms behind the Ancestral Female Trauma: nature and nurture.

Nature refers to DNA. Study after study confirms that any kind of trauma (war, rape, miscarriage, drowning, domestic violence...) is biologically inherited to following generations. Think about it; traumatic experiences of your mom and grandma are alive in your genes. Have you experienced irrational fears and thoughts? This could be an explanation.

A common story I hear from my female customers is their terror of speaking up. Being visible, expressing their true thoughts, terrifies them. They feel suffocated, their throats closing and their whole body sweating. Any resemblance to the experience of burning witches? Could this be one of this trauma inherited experiences? Could it be?

Now let's explore nurture. Environment, upbringing, and life experience determine our behavior and destiny. Stories, 'normal' cultural practices, arguments, sayings, cultural structures, political environments, religious ideas and more, 'nurture' this trauma from uterus to death bed.

Think about the stories you heard and hear about women and money. For example: 'she's a gold digger'. When you were a child this added to your unconscious programming beliefs like:

- Receiving money is bad
- Being sexually expressive is bad
- Being beautiful is bad

Now think about 'normal' practices in your country. Let's take: 'women do most of the unpaid care activities'. This reinforces your programing adding beliefs like:

- Well-groomed children have a good mother
- A clean home is the responsibility of a good mother
- Nourishing is the responsibility of a good mother

These are just a few of the many non-supportive beliefs that compose the Ancestral Female Trauma. As you can perhaps identify, they are highly contradictory and loaded with painful feelings.

Of course, if we don't heal it we will pass it on to the next generations, together with its devastating effects. As we have been ignoring it, this is what's been happening for centuries. It's time to change history. You and I are the ones who will be doing so.

Don't despair! There's hope. Even if this has been repeating itself for centuries, the whole global consciousness is raising. We are the generation that's healing this centuries-old problem. We are awakening to the fact that wholeness, health, and abundance are our true identity.

How to heal the Ancestral Female Trauma

The main reason why the AFT keeps alive in each one of us for generations is because we pretend it doesn't exist. We just don't talk about it. It hurts too much. We get locked into a self-destructive drama that includes:

- Creating the us versus them story
- Acting either (excessively) strong or helpless
- Desiring justice or revenge
- Hiding painful feelings: sadness, fear, shame, guilt
- Becoming the 'Queen Bee': hard, aggressive, insensitive, violent

As you gathered by my personal story, I was totally immersed in this drama. In the first chapter of my life, my AFT lead me to 'fierceness'. I hid my fragility in the suit of 'the Type A woman'. Then, in the second chapter of my life, my AFT was still running my life. I just hid it under a different dress: the 'poor me', damsel in distress outfit.

I had to touch rock bottom to finally decide to face my own traumatic origins. It was only when I was unable to function (having a shower was too much at that point!), that I decided to get into my personal story. This doesn't need to happen to you.

You just need to decide. Decisions are powerful, life-changing keys. The wise Tony Robbins says: "your life changes the moment you make a new, congruent, and committed decision."

Once you make the decision to break the chain of inherited pain, for you and for the generations to come, the tools are there for you. They are easy but not simple. They demand courage and determination.

I can tell you I still have my weak moments, when I let the old programming sadden me. However, when I see the face of my daughter and of other younger women, I double down on my own self-worth healing practices.

Conclusion

So, how would you now react when you read the horrible statistics of women and money? Still feeling anger or helpless? Or maybe something else?

A Call to Action!

What about seeing yourself as the powerful spirit that is untouched by all that drama? What about seeing yourself as the spirit that will bring reconciliation with the past generations and hope for the next ones?

I invite you to break the cycle of soul wounding. I invite you to express your feelings, not to repress them. I invite you to accept what happened to you and to your ancestors. Take the risk of looking at the uncomfortable story of the feminine. Take the risk of working with 'them'. Take the risk of understating 'their' story.

Take the risk of healing your own soul wounds. The rewards are immense. The inspiring role model and leader within will be unleashed.

Footnotes

1 https://inequality.org/gender-inequality/#gender-income-gaps

2 https://www.nirsonline.org/2016/03/women-80-more-likely-to-be-impoverished-in-retirement/

3 https://www.marketwatch.com/story/women-regret-this-financial-mistake-the-most-2018-04-19

4 http://agewave.com/what-we-do/landmark-research-and-consulting/research-studies/women-and-financial-wellness/

16

Melissa Raczak

***Melissa Raczak** has been with Deloitte for over 20 years. She is a Partner within the ET&P Practice and part of the Technology, Media, and Telecom industry team. She is also an executive coach and certified Inclusive Leadership coach. For over six years, she led the Deloitte Netherlands Women's Networking Group.*

In our current environment, with much of the global workplace displaced from the office and working remotely, burnout is a real issue. We are not so much working from home, as we are living in the office. But burnout can occur at any point in your career and knowing the signs and signals is critically important. In her essay, Melissa shares her personal story of experiencing burnout, what she learned, and how it shaped her career.

Melissa is an American who moved to the Netherlands for love: Dutch love. She is married, with 2 daughters in their late teens.

→ *To contact Melissa: linkedin.com/in/melissaraczak*

Preventing Burnout and Managing Well-Being

Hitting the proverbial wall and experiencing burnout, at a pivotal time in your career, is NOT something you want to experience. Trust me!

I've been there, done that, and worn that T-shirt. It was a difficult time in my life but it also gave much back to me. I came to realize what I wanted for myself and, in the end, I came out a better professional, mother, wife, daughter, and friend.

Deeper and deeper

In 2010, I was a Director at Deloitte and seemingly had it all: a great job, nice house and cars, a supportive partner, and two healthy children. But in reality, I was running with the pedal to the metal and didn't realize I was burning out. I was sleep deprived for years. I'd been working a reduced work week but really ended up doing 5 to 6 days of work in 4 days. I was burdened by feelings of guilt of not being a good enough mother, spouse, and colleague. I had difficulty saying no to things and took on more and more responsibility, wanting to be liked and to please everyone. I could not mentally shut off my brain and would lie in bed awake for hours with my mind racing. Or I would wake up from the stress several hours before my alarm clock went off and not be able to calm my mind. Over time, I slowly started to break down. At first, physically. The year before my burnout, I was ill much of the time and regularly on antibiotics. I started to feel drained of energy. I was physically exhausted and tried to motivate myself to get out of bed each day, just to get going. Every evening I struggled to gather the energy to care for my 6 and 7 year old daughters, and by Friday evening I was wiped out. The only things I was ready for were to sit on the couch or go to bed. I had never experienced or understood what depression was, but that was exactly where burnout had led me.

Asking for help

I knew I needed help but asking for help can be very difficult. Firstly, I was embarrassed and ashamed. Secondly, I thought it would be career limiting if I raised a flag that I was exhausted and it was all too much. And thirdly, I didn't know who to turn to or where to go. The turning point came one day when I drove to the office, but I couldn't make myself go inside. A previous client lived a few minutes from the office, and I knew I needed to speak with someone. I went to her house and broke down. She referred me to someone to talk to and that got the ball rolling towards healing myself.

Through my recovery process, which included a four-and-a-half-month career break from Deloitte, I learned that recognizing the signs and signals of burnout is critically important. The World Health Organization defines burnout as a syndrome that results from chronic workplace stress that has not been successfully managed. It's an occupational phenomenon that is characterized by:

- feelings of energy depletion or exhaustion;
- increased mental distance from one's job, or feelings of negativism or cynicism related to one's job;
- and reduced professional efficacy (connection).
- Most people who are experiencing burnout will continue working and not even realize they are dealing with it. Instead, they think they're struggling to manage difficult and stressful times. But if you are feeling fatigued, irritable, have lowered levels of motivation and vitality, increased frustration, or are spending more time working, with less being accomplished, then you may be experiencing burnout.

Some of the lies we tell ourselves to deal with these feelings are:
- I am fine
- I love my job
- I am just tired
- I will rest this weekend
- People are depending on me
- I'll take a vacation and be okay
- I'll be fine once this is done and things get back to normal

Believing these statements is okay. However, denying that the current situation is damaging to your well-being and not recognizing that changes need to be made, is truly detrimental to your physical and mental health. Change is driven by awareness. Once you are aware, you can become motivated. But you have to be motivated to act and do something differently.

Recovery

After my career break, I considered stepping out of my career. As I continued through the recovery process, I started back at Deloitte part-time and built myself back up again. The neuroplasticity of the brain allows us to develop new neural connections and pathways. Old habits can be unlearned, just as new ones can become imbedded. I learned so much about myself during this time and it was an eye-opening experience. I tried all kinds of things that I thought were ridiculous before: coaching, mindfulness, meditation, the power of breathing, becoming conscious of my thoughts; were they serving or supporting me? Or were they hindering me? I opened myself up to new experiences and gained insight in this self-discovery journey. What I learned, is that there is a framework for well-being comprised of four elements: physical, mental, emotional, and spiritual. They all need to be addressed.

- Start with bringing your body back into balance. Are you eating well? Are you getting the right amount and quality of sleep? Are you exercising if able to do so? If you don't do these things, then everything else can be impacted. When experiencing burnout, many

people first run to a mental coach, but you cannot address those core issues if your energy is depleted.
- Once physical stability is achieved, then focus on the mental. What are the thoughts running through your head? Are they serving you? Are you worrying about things too much and feeling overwhelmed or helpless? Don't let worry hijack you. Prepare, try to live in the moment, deal with things as they happen, and move on.
- The next step is emotional. How frustrated do you get with people or circumstances? Does missing the train ruin your day? Embrace every situation, the good and the bad. Look for the positive in everything. Tap into your emotions, be aware of them, and what you are doing in response. We can control our emotions and up our happiness quotient or we can stay in a really negative space. The decision is in our power.
- Once the physical, mental, and emotional are in balance, then the final element is spiritual. I define spiritual as your connection to yourself, others, and your work. If the other elements are aligned, then you can clearly see and evaluate your personal and professional relationships. A lot of people are unhappy in their careers and want to flee, but if you break it down, you will see that the job is not the issue. Exhaustion, fatigue, and burnout are the core problems. Jumping into another job isn't going to solve anything and is not going to provide long term fulfilment.

Everyday actions

As you work on these four elements, there are everyday actions you can take to change embedded, destructive behaviors that contribute to burnout:
- Ask yourself: am I doing the things I want to be doing? Is this taking me a step forward?
- Drink enough water and don't live on caffeine
- Build breaks in your day to reenergize yourself. Everyone needs to get up and move every 90 minutes.
- After difficult conversations, do what I call the 'Zebra Shake' where you shake your whole body for 1 minute. This shakes off the anxiety, frustration, and stress of the situation.

- Reflect at the end of your day. Try journaling for a month. Ask yourself questions like: What went well today and why? What didn't go well today and how could it have gone better? What were my stress signs and signals? What is my energy level on a scale of 1 through 10?
- And one last tip is the power of breathing; it changes the whole chemical balance in your body. Learn a breathing technique and do it for 1 to 5 minutes, multiple times a day. The power of breathing is transformative. It can calm and energize you at the same time.

The burnout I experienced 10 years ago was a very challenging time, but it taught me so much. It helped me to get clearer on what I wanted for myself and it motivated me to become a partner at Deloitte. If I had continued on the path I was on and not sought help, I can honestly say I would have left Deloitte. I can even say that I am now thankful for this dip in my life because it brought me so many insights.

A Call to Action!

In conclusion, remember that personal success, and feeling healthy and energetic is something we all want. But if life is not in balance, our energy level goes down and everything else with it. Spend time on understanding your purpose, build self-confidence, and flourish in your strength zone. And finally, always look out for your well-being. Look out for yourself and take care of each other.

17

Ana Herrero-Wallace

***Ana Herrero-Wallace** has lived in 5 countries (Spain, US, Hungary, UK, NL). At 22, she started as one of the first women stock traders in the US, to finish in London and Amsterdam working in Financial Technology. After a sabbatical in Australia, she began her own startup in 2019, My Mindful Money, with the aim to engage, inspire, and encourage women to manage their money mindfully and make empowered investment decisions. As for her personal portfolio, she owns real estate, has over 20 years of stock market investment experience, and is planning for early retirement at 50.*

She is also mother to two children. Ana started on the board of PWN (Professional Women Network.) NL as VP Finance and, since the spring of 2021, as President. She persuades women to start investing and to start talking about money, as women learn best when speaking to each other.

→ *To contact Ana: linkedin.com/in/ana-herrero-wallace*
facebook.com/mymindfulmoneyblogs

How Every Woman Can Start Investing

Once upon a time, there was a young girl growing up in Madrid. That girl was me. Fear regarding money started when I was a teenager. My father, at the age of 50, had lost his job. My family's financial situation changed very quickly. We went from having expensive ski trips to a time of anxiety, all overnight. My father struggled to find employment, while my mother, who was a housewife, had little to no prospects.

Luckily, my parents had been very cautious with money, investing, and saving. We were able to live off their savings for a few years until they opened a small company. I now realize that my life had changed forever, especially my feelings towards money and the importance of savings and investments.

A couple of decades later, despite my teenage drama with money, I find myself in the best financial situation ever. I own several investment properties and have been investing in the stock market for the past two decades. This is not to brag but more to let you know: it is doable. Even living on an average income, by people with little financial education and a financial trauma, such as myself.

I am most proud to be able to share my experiences to help many women be successful in their investment journeys. In 2019, I created a small start-up to help inspire women, as most who have encountered had never spoken about their finances to friends or partners. My company is built on empowering women to learn more about their personal finances and how to achieve more.

The biggest discovery I made during my coaching sessions, was how dearly the taboo against talking about money has cost women. Not only have women been disenfranchised for years, they also have been kept from one of the primary ways they learn: by talking to one another. The taboo remains firmly in place, despite having made strides in the workplace and having more control over our own money. My purpose is to break this taboo. Women are being empowered to both making decisions about their finances and managing them.

Owning your personal finances

We live in a world that until very recently, thought a woman's financial place was to be dependent on men. Women were relying on male partners, fathers, or male financial advisors to handle their financial affairs. Relying on others is not only unhealthy but can also cost women dearly. It is beneficial to develop your own skills and learn some basics which will make you self-reliant.

However, like our muscles, we must exercise these skills repeatedly in order to strengthen our financial character. There will be times when you lose money and that is OK, even expected. I have lost a lot, yet I have also gained a lot more over the longer term. The more I invest, the better I get at it.

I experienced plenty of machismo throughout my financial services career. I worked as a trader in the US and then on a trading floor in Budapest. Unlike the US, where I had a few female colleagues, in Hungary I was not just the only foreigner but also the only woman. I dealt with the pressure of being told by my colleagues I should find a husband, quit my job, and start a family. I must have been extremely hard of hearing, as I didn't take their advice until many years later.

However, you don't need to feel like you had to work in financial services or as a trader like myself, in order to perform well in the stock market. Warwick Business School conducted a study of nearly 3,000 UK men and women[1] investing in the stock market and tracking their performance over three years. Not only did the women do better than men by 1.8 percentage points, but they also outperformed the UK main stock index, the FTSE 100. The same study also focused on the number of times women trade versus men. Women trade an average of 9 times per year in the market versus 13 for men. For this reason, men tend to incur higher fees from trading, which can erode returns over time.

Work for money or let money work for you?

The best financial move I ever made was to create a financial plan. Do not dismiss the idea just yet; it is useful even if you think you are still too young or that it's boring. Many women have a career plan, a wedding plan, but not a plan for retirement and what steps need to be taken now to achieve those plans. Both my husband and I want to retire no later than our mid-50's, not rich but wealthy enough to be comfortable. Everything I do today is to fulfil that goal in the future.

How did I achieve my perceived financial comfort? Why do I think this is possible for anyone? The amount of money you earn is (somewhat) irrelevant. It is more about how much money you invest and less about your earning record.

Saving is also important if you want to have something left over to invest. Most importantly, you need to focus on where your income is coming from. This is paramount for financial independence. A few years ago, I realized that if I only kept my corporate job as a source of income, I would never become financially independent. For me, this represents earning enough money from your passive investments, so that you do not really have to have a full-time job to sustain yourself. My husband and I plan to live off our passive investments, while holding a part time job to supplement our expenses.

There are two types of income. The first is money made in exchange for work, i.e. earned via employment or by being self-employed. The second type is leveraged or passive income, which is the one that is not proportional to the amount of time you put into work. This can be any of the following: rental income (which I started doing in 2015), selling some sort of product online that is downloaded repeatedly (which I do not have yet), or dividends earned from stocks (which I have received for decades now). Basically, this is money you make while sleeping. In most cases, unless you start acting and receiving passive income, you will find it difficult to achieve financial independence.

There is another point that benefits those who look for passive income. In most countries like the Netherlands, UK, and the US, investors are favored and savers are not. In addition, almost everywhere, we are highly taxed on our income but not so much on investment income from stocks and rental income from real estate. When you earn passive money, in many cases you get to keep it all for yourself!

My top 6 tips for investment beginners

I recommend the following to my clients, after we have looked at their personal situation in terms of bad debt, like credit card debt. This should be paid off before you even think about starting to invest.

1. **Separate piggy banks.** Separate your 'emergency fund' from your investment. Meaning, if you need money at hand for an emergency, it's better not to invest it and keep it as cash on hand. That way, you can access it immediately without having to worry about its value and how to minimize loss.
2. **Start early and invest consistently.** Start investing as soon as possible: time is your friend and will allow you to compound your money. You might be tempted to think you have to have a lot of time and you'd rather wait until tomorrow to start investing. Although stock markets can go up and down, making regular investments and reinvesting the dividends, makes you more likely to ride out volatility, allowing the long-term effects that compound interest has in your investments.

3. **Invest in index funds and have a diversified portfolio.** Your investment is composed of a diverse number of countries and industries. This allows you to decrease risk. I have a good mixture of US, European and Emerging markets, which include Asia and Latin America, in my stock portfolio. In addition, I invest heavily in low costs trackers or index funds, like the S&P500 (which replicates the S&P500 US index).
4. **Avoid buying individual shares of stocks.** However, if you wish to do that, make sure you invest in companies you understand. If you want to invest in individual stocks, make sure this is only around 10% of your investments. Never invest 10% of your portfolio in just one stock and try not to own more than 5% of stock in the company you work at, to diminish risk. Oftentimes, the stocks can move up or down too much, versus an index fund which is a lot more stable.
5. **Think long term.** Only invest money in the market you do not need in the next 5 years. Short term investing is a recipe for disaster. Always buy in a regular pattern. You will make money if you have time in the market, not by trying to time it.
6. **Be frugal in paying unnecessary fees for your investing.** Use low costs funds like Vanguard and Ishares. If you use a financial advisor, think twice about how much value they are providing. Make sure they are only charging a fixed fee for their time and not a commission on your portfolio or every time you trade. Always inquire about fees with them. Don't be shy; be ruthless. This is your hard-earned money we are talking about, after all.

Don't be a risk taker

In my opinion, you are already a risk taker if you are doing nothing with your money except allowing it to just sit in your bank account. While it just sits in your savings account, it's worth less every year due to inflation. Also, you are losing the opportunity costs of investing that money, plus the opportunity of making your investment muscle stronger by practicing investing right now.

Studies have shown women are less likely to invest or to open a trading account than men. According to the Financial Times, Interactive

Investor, which is an online brokerage, showed that only 1 in 4 online trading accounts belong to a woman. As a financial coach, I also know that women are good about putting money into a savings account but less good in putting it into investments that grow their money. Just remember: the biggest risk of all is taking no risk.

A Call to Action!

Here are some tips on how you can help the women around you become better with their finances.

If you are lucky enough to already have investments and feel like a pro at this game, please share your stories. Keep in mind that your friend might be scared when you make recommendations, after you share with her your financial failures and successes. She might need more time to research things before she decides to invest like you do.

- Provide the resources, so she can do the research.
- Make sure you provide a safe environment, so she can freely ask you the 'stupid' questions.
- Encourage your friends to read financial books and learn.

I also recommend we start sharing our stories! Look at joining an investment club or social financial club on social media, to network with others. I am a member of many and have made many friendships with likeminded women. Joining personal finance groups on Facebook has helped me learn from others.

If you are on the receiving side of the stories and still have little experience investing, then be open to your fears. Don't be afraid to ask and reach out to other people whose financial decisions you admire. You can learn about why and how they bought that house, etc. Working hard might not make you financially independent but working smart will, and then we will all live happily ever after.

Footnotes

[1] Warwick Business School website- https://www.wbs.ac.uk/news/are-women-better-investors-than-men/

18 Dr. Margarita Lourido

__Dr. Margarita Lourido__ has lived, studied, and worked in several countries. She holds a Cum Laude Ph.D. in Clinical Psychology from Barcelona University. She is the founder of Switch Intercultural and works as a success psychologist for internationals, facilitating their personal and professional development.

She promotes compassionate success because, for her, there is no success without taking care of yourself and being your authentic self. She is passionate about using her knowledge and life experience to support international professionals who decide they're going to write their own stories. The people who know deep down that they can make a great impact on this world; the ones who decide their aspirations are going to take them far from home.

→ *To contact Margarita: linkedin.com/in/dr-margarita-lourido-success-psychologist | switchintercultural.com*

Finding Joy and Succeeding in Difficult Situations

It was dawn and a startling noise awoke me. I sat up in bed in the dark, my heart pounding. I took in slow deep breaths to calm myself, touching my face, my arms, my torso, looking for any trace of blood. I couldn't find any. Thanks to the streetlights, I could see that everything seemed normal in my room. As my panic faded, I came to the conclusion that the noise had been a bomb exploding, a not infrequent occurrence. I said to myself: 'there is nothing to do right now, tomorrow is a school day, go back to sleep'. And I slept.

When I was growing up in Cali, Colombia, the drug cartels had a big impact on everyday life. In the 1980s and 1990s, civilians in Colombia were either observers or victims of the armed conflict between the cartels, guerrillas, paramilitaries, and the army. Violence was part of our reality, and we were forced to live with it. We developed emotional coping mechanisms and daily practices to minimize the pain flooding the country and to get on with our lives.

In fact, if you ask me, I can only say that I had a happy childhood and adolescence in Colombia. You might think that experiencing these things would have been terrifying, but it was our normal. It was a given that personal safety was not guaranteed. When we couldn't drive out of the city to enjoy the countryside because it was too dangerous, we learned to enjoy safe places in the city. I instinctively learned to focus my attention on the good in life, even when I was constantly witnessing a dark side of it. I learned to be happy and grateful with the simple wonders available.

Recognizing contrast

In 2002, after gaining some work experience as a psychologist, I decided to continue my career abroad in Barcelona. It was a late winter evening, chilly, though not too cold. I went out for dinner with friends, and we were saying goodbye, ready to go back home. We had talked so warmly, and I felt so relaxed and comfortable that I had this feeling of 'I don't want this moment to end'. It was after 11 pm and we were standing on one of the corners of Plaça de Catalunya. There were all kinds of people walking around us: tourists, locals, and the occasional drunk. At that moment, I felt a warm sensation in my chest and my heart filled with happiness. I had a feeling that I hadn't felt before. I realized I was laughing and talking, without worrying about staying alert and continually checking my surroundings for danger.

I realized I was on the street, late at night, and I felt safe!
I felt free.

If emotions are the wisdom of the body, my body was giving me a clear sign. I knew that I was going to create opportunities that would allow me to feel peace and freedom in my life.

Life is contrast

The contrast gives us clarity; it allows us to see our path to grow in life.

How is it possible that standing on the street on a winter night can be such a wonderful thing? The contrast between living in fear for years and enjoying a moment of tranquility, allowed this feeling to flourish. My interpretation of this moment made it special; the ordinary became extraordinary. For many years, unconsciously, I had not experienced peace around me; I didn't have the space to feel free. The lack of this tranquility led me to deeply appreciate something as simple as being outside on the street with friends. Knowing the difference between going outside in fear and enjoying going out without fear, gave me the clarity of wanting a new experience. Knowing that there is a reality where security is not guaranteed, gave me the motivation to seek the security I needed.

Life is contrast. There are things we like and there are things we dislike. Some situations are pleasant for us, and others are painful for us. And through this variety of things and situations, we can discover our identity, our dreams, and our path to walk ahead. We create a clear vision of what we want to experience.

Let me share with you some questions to recognize contrast and its benefits:

- Do you remember a difficult situation in your life and the pain generated from this situation?
- Do you remember how, from this situation, you began to want something different in your life?
- Do you remember how this desire led you to make a decision, to take action, and to grow?

For example:

- A bad work experience may have prompted you to make a career change that aligns better with your talents.
- Burnout may have forced you to be compassionate to yourself and you learned to respect your limits.
- Maybe a bad relationship helped you define new priorities in your life.
- An accident may have put you in touch with your resilience.

Yes, we all know these types of situations lead to accelerated growth. The contrast between health and illness makes us desire to be fit and motivates us to take action to achieve vitality. This is how we grow in life. For this reason, I decided a couple of years ago to stop classifying situations in categories such as good or bad. Categorizing and judging a situation prevents us from seeing available solutions. It robs us of opportunities. If we can take a broad perspective on life, then every situation supports us, even if it is painful or uncomfortable. A challenging situation shows you the way to grow. If you are willing to listen, see, reflect, and look at yourself, you will realize that each experience brings clarity, strength, and well-being.

Appreciation as a lifehack

Appreciation brings us joy, diminishes the pain and discomfort of contrast, and is the key to having our happiness in our hands.
If contrast is necessary in our life, we know that, sooner or later, an unpleasant situation is bound to occur. We can face it in fear or remorse. Or we can look for joy and peace.

Think of what you do when a difficult situation comes into your life:
- Do you recognize the value of this experience?
- What do you do to return to your natural state of joy, when you are in the middle of a difficult situation?

When you are in these kinds of situations, the fastest way out of a negative spiral of thoughts is appreciation. Appreciation is the act of opening a door to reframe your problem and find solutions.

Finding solutions through appreciation

In my practice as a success psychologist and coach for internationals, many clients come to me with a situation they want to change immediately, as it is quite uncomfortable.

So, I ask them:
- What exactly do you want to change in this situation?
- What is your ideal situation?

And I also ask them:
- What can you find in the current situation that is or was good for you?
- How is this situation supporting you to build the future you want?

These last two questions are not easy to answer. However, as an answer begins to form, the discomfort begins to diminish and solutions begin to bloom. When we appreciate the beauty that exists even in difficult situations, they cease to affect us drastically. This is what I call, 'stepping off the roller coaster'.

Ask yourself: what can I appreciate from this difficult situation? Simply by posing the question to yourself, you shift your focus from what is wrong, to what is good and helpful in this situation.

For instance, the Covid-19 pandemic has led to chaos, stress, a greater workload, or uncertainty for many in their professional lives. Despite these conditions, you can reflect on this situation and, through appreciation, you can reconnect with the aspects of the work you love. Through appreciating the contribution you are making in people's lives, you will find a way to have a different experience. An experience you can enjoy, despite the circumstances. An experience you can choose.

This is the time when your joy does not depend on the results of a situation. It does not depend on the good mood of your colleagues or boss; nor does it depend on the stress levels of your partner. Your joy depends on your willingness to see a different reality and to appreciate the moment you are living.

Where the ordinary becomes extraordinary

- Appreciation for the beauty that exists in difficult situations allowed me to have a happy childhood, even while living in a time of armed conflict.
- Appreciation for the connection and freedom I felt in Barcelona allowed me to choose a path in which peace is a priority.
- Appreciation for personal evolution motivates me to help professional internationals to grow at a personal and professional level, by taking care of themselves and following their dreams.
- Appreciation for differences has allowed me to have a wonderful multicultural marriage and life abroad.

Appreciation makes me more human, makes me feel a greater connection with the people around me, makes me enjoy my work, and gives me joy every day.

A Call to Action!

Explore your experience. In self-reflection, you will find your power. Now tell me, in your career as an entrepreneur or as a corporate professional:

- Do you want to change a situation?
- Can you see how contrast is giving you clarity?
- What will you choose to appreciate today?

Remember, you always have a choice. Choose the perspective that will support your happiness and success.

19 Caroline van Leuven

__Caroline van Leuven__ has a rich working experience in the private and public sector, as well as an entrepreneur. She started her career leading the documentation service desks at Deloitte and the financial department of the Ministry of General Affairs.

She's an independent management consultant for more than 25 years. Since 2005, she's been a (board) member of the Professional Women's Network, having served for circa 5 years as VP and President.

After a post-graduate study in psychology at the Goodfield Institute in 2007, Caroline combined business coaching and consultancy. In addition, she set-up the Women in Society Foundation which supports women in vulnerable positions to achieve economic independence. She also serves as a board member in a family investment fund, facilitating medical research. Through the economic crisis caused by the pandemic, Caroline worked for a government sponsored initiative, coaching and supporting entrepreneurs and executives in various fields. Her focus was on helping them develop a deeper self-awareness to gain insights into changes that could be made.

→ *To contact Caroline: linkedin.com/in/carolinevanleuven*
indivisible.nl

Networking is an Art

In the mid-80s, I graduated from the Amsterdam University of Applied Sciences, in the field of documentary information for companies. I was approached almost immediately for a job: collecting information for an international institute that mapped conference and congress activities worldwide.

The invitation came because I was the only one who didn't shy away from applying for a job in English. Back then, that was still unique; nowadays, in many companies, the working language in the Netherlands is English. Incidentally, I didn't get the job because the director thought I was too ambitious for this position. What I mainly gained were interesting conversations with the director of the organization and the head of the department. In these conversations, I became aware of the first principles of networking.

The first steps

Shortly afterwards, I got my first permanent job at the Nederlandse Accountantsmaatschap, which is now known as Deloitte. I became responsible for the documentation center which supported the Amsterdam advisory practice for accountants, tax consultants, and management consultants. I thought it sounded very prestigious; it was also really fun, but it actually sounded more impressive than it was.

Now, years later, I can proudly say that I expanded my local department at the Amsterdam office into a support department. Not only for all Dutch offices but also for the international affiliated offices which needed information from the Netherlands. And that in a time, when fax and email didn't exist. Communication took place by telephone, traditional mail, or telex. I spoke to the advisers personally. In doing this, I learned their way of working, their interests, what I should be alert to, and what was interesting for them. I was able to do favors (both asked and not asked for) and help many colleagues. Justifiably, I was proud of the results, learning how to trade PR and establish my reputation, in a positive manner. Without knowing it at the time, these were my first actual networking steps.

The first women's network

In the mid-1980s, hardly any official business women's networks existed. There was a secretarial network and there was the rural women's association. But a network for business women to join, such as men were able to do, didn't exist.

That changed when an women's network was set up in Amsterdam, available for women who worked in international organizations. Meetings were held in the Hilton Hotel at Schiphol. A group of internationally working women needed contacts with like-minded people. The network offered them this opportunity.

Despite the fact that I had a good job and met the requirements for membership, I didn't feel comfortable when I attended meetings. I was just out of college. In the network, I was surrounded by a group of successful women who had been working internationally for more than 20 years and certainly were 20 years older than me. I saw a great amount of experience and didn't feel I fit in. It felt safer to stay with the associations related to my work, where my knowledge was superior. Of course, looking back, it was a completely wrong reason to drop out of the network. I can only now guess as to how these women would have enriched my personal and professional life.

A chance comment

In 2005, I was studying psychology. My professor shared that he had recently given a speech for an international women's network. I was curious and decided to find out if this was the same network I had been a part of back in the 80's. It was, and I was surprised when I realized that, in the meantime, the Amsterdam network had become part of a large European network, with its own digital platform. The founding cities of the 1980s had united into an international platform. I signed up, was warmly welcomed, and have been a member ever since. It became a new school for me.

Even though I felt I was always careful in the steps I took, being a member of PWN made me aware of social skills I had never thought about before. And not only that, there was also concern for the members. If I hadn't been to meetings for a while, I would get a call, checking if everything was okay because they hadn't seen me in a while. There was a real effort to get and keep me involved.

I had now been self-employed for several years, working for interesting clients. Like many other independent entrepreneurs, I found customer acquisition difficult and realized how important it was to have contacts. And how do you get contacts? By networking.

After being a member of the network (known then as the European Professional Women's Network or EPWN) for about two years, I was asked if I was interested in a board position. The position of VP Membership became available.

I took on the challenge because I realized that with this role, I could really make a difference for members. And that decision brought me a lot; by attentively welcoming each member, it resulted in many recommendations for new members. What was also special, is I got to know a lot of people at a personal and professional level.

In my work, I was alert to connect information with a certain logic. In my board role, this also became interesting and applicable in contacts between people. Each member has her own story. As the VP

Membership, I had access to a lot of information and I was able to give meaning to it. This was very interesting and it gave my networking skills a huge boost, which helps me tremendously in my work to this day.

Next level networking

When the role of chairman of the network came open, I grabbed it with both hands. Networking went to the next level for me. Together with fellow board members, we gave presentations to companies to recruit members. We explained the benefits of membership and how you could especially reap the benefits personally.

I've always taken the view that being a member of a network doesn't just mean showing up every now and then because there's a nice event with an interesting speaker. PWN (as the network is now called) has, and had, a large platform with a decent database of international members. Joining as a member, you are able to take advantage of that too. I always found it incomprehensible that we had to explain so emphatically how important this was and what an advantage a membership also gave you. After all, one of our biggest motivations was to facilitate women in their next career step. It was not just about themes such as diversity and women to the top; it was not just about organizing inspiring events. The network can also be seen as a large playing field to learn things, to make contacts, to practice and to ask for help if you need it.

With the online platform, it is visible in advance to see which members had registered for which event. An important lesson in this was to be aware of how you prepare for such an evening: which contacts could be important for what was going on in your work or company at that time.

Networking is real work: preparing and reflecting on what you will get and what you will bring. In my role, I also found it interesting to connect people internationally or at least to make use of the possibilities. There was one member who had an ambitious goal to internationally promote the company she worked for. Whenever she went to travel to a city where there was a PWN sister network, I introduced her to the local chairperson or VP Membership. She had a great time and made interesting contacts.

By being alert and staying on top of things, complicated issues suddenly turned out to be solvable for members because I could provide them with a contact. That is a big advantage if you are a member of such a network as this. And being a board member can give you that extra boost.

Your career development

Many interesting speakers at our events provide valuable lessons in developing yourself for your next career step. You must have clear goals, otherwise contacts and a network are of no use to you. Know what you are bringing and know what you are coming to get. Prepare well for every step you take. Networking is an important part of your career preparation and progression.

And, if your career is an important step for you, coordinate it well with the home front. A career starts at the kitchen table by coordinating your ambitions with your partner. A career is partly determined by the home front: do you let it support you or hold you back? Many highly educated women with good incomes, even earning more than their partner, start working less or even stop completely when they become mothers. They don't consider the consequences for advancing their career. It's not easy, but it's not impossible, to chart your own course with vision. You can create your own success when you have children.

Good networking is an art. It takes years of practice and becoming aware to constantly act on what is needed: fulfilling commitments, fulfilling promises, and seeing opportunities and possibilities. How nice is it, if you can contribute to improve not only your life but the lives of others as well? You will be a happier person for it. It's so easy, as long as you remember that it's also work. It's 'just'-working.

A Call to Action!

Prepare yourself: be aware what you want to achieve visiting an event and set a goal. This counts for every business meeting. Your time is valuable, so make the most of it. Find out background information of those you are going to meet. Ask yourself what you want to achieve and what you bring to the table to support others. And if you want to be sure someone you want to meet is there, send him or her an invite beforehand.

- Take your business cards and other information you want to give away, with you. Do this in time before you leave the office or the house.
- Learn to listen with an open mind: ask questions, connect the dots in your mind, and show interest in the other attendees.
- Step up for yourself: dare to introduce yourself and tell your story. Do not wait or hesitate; your time is limited in a conversation.
- Be open to new possibilities and dare to step out of your comfort zone.
- If you make a promise to someone, act upon it within 24 to 48 hours after the meeting, otherwise you'll forget. If you get an introduction or contact by someone else, act upon it also within 24 to 48 hours, to keep the energy going.
- Learn to deal with disappointments. If something is not going your way, find another way to make it happen. Perseverance is key in your behavior.
- Enjoy, smile, and learn. Networking is working too!
- It is an art and a skill. Learn to master the art of networking!

20

Sheila Gemin

***Sheila Gemin** is a massive fan of Star Wars. In Star Wars, technology, diversity, and energy come together in the galaxy to protect peace between different life forms and planets. A great analogy.*

I believe when technology, and a diversity of skills and experiences come together, magic will happen. We will be able to protect the future of our children and sustain our planet.

Sheila Gemin is a mother of four. She is a huge fan of science fiction and fantasy and an engineer working in an IT leadership role within the largest bank of the Netherlands, ING. Having started out in the field of technology with an international consulting firm, she has over 20 years' experience as corporate professional working in Tech and Finance. This, while starting, building, and selling a company focusing on athletic development and charity. In the last five years, Sheila has been President of PWN NL and PWN Global.

→ *To contact Sheila: linkedin.com/in/sheilagemin*

A Next Phase for D&I

Diversity and inclusion are now, more than ever, a topic on organizations' and leaders' agendas across society. Having a D&I officer or someone vocal about the D&I strategy in your organization is the new normal. If I look back on my career, this is something new. When I started working in IT, women working as IT consultants were scarce. No D&I officers existed.

I like this shift. In the last 10-15 years, this D&I movement has become one of the cornerstones in the corporate world. I believe it positively impacts women, people of color, and people of the LBGTQ+ community. There are no quotas in place, and there is a clear ambition to have a more diverse workforce.

My ideas about diversity and inclusion are now moving on to the next phase. There is a solid call to action from men and women to be more diverse and inclusive. The reality is that the current need for action was to have more women in leadership ranks. This resulted in more women entering the leadership ranks; to be more precise, white women. Taking a closer look at the PWN community and leadership, it is safe to say there are enough women, but diversity in terms of color or religion is not so visible. We can work on this.

PWN Global is an inclusive community which now welcomes men and women from many backgrounds. Our primary focus is to accelerate gender-balanced leadership in business and society. Yet, we have never really addressed that women with different skin color or cultural backgrounds may face additional career development challenges and opportunities.

Are they really diverse and inclusive?

In (social) media, you often come across organizations that pride themselves on being diverse and inclusive. If you take a closer look, you will see teams composed of only white women or a mixture of white men and women. In both instances, I question their claim to be 'diverse'. For me, diversity goes beyond gender and culture.

From a professional point of view, it is hard to find women of color in leadership positions. I know they are there; just not very visible and highly under-represented in the female leadership space. According to an HBR report, women of color represent 4% of C-level positions, falling far below white men (68%) and white women (19%).

Another study found that women of color are most likely to experience workplace harassment amongst all groups. They are often held to a much higher standard than their white and male peers. And they are frequently presumed to be less qualified, despite their credentials, work skills, or business results. Perhaps even more alarming, they receive less support from their managers, according to the same McKinsey and Leanin.org study. They are less likely to have bosses who promote their work contributions to others, help them navigate organizational politics, or socialize with them outside of work. Thus, they're often left out of the informal networks that propel most high-potentials forward in their careers. They lack the kind of meaningful mentoring and sponsorship that is critical for getting ahead.

As a woman of color, I am stereotyped in many ways and judged on my appearance. I have been seen as the nanny (of my children), the assistant, or the intern. Also, I have been complimented on my ability to speak fluent Dutch (Dutch is my mother tongue) and criticized because I do not cook, nor like spices and peppers. I have been called a savage and a tropical surprise. People seem to be quite astonished when they find out I am an engineer in the technology industry. The latter rightly, because in general, women in technology are also under-represented.

So, what's new?

Nothing. It is essential to mention that both men AND women stereotype one another: we judge/discriminate and make assumptions based on appearance. It is not a man's problem. Being inclusive towards people who do not look like you, even if the gender is the same, is a prerequisite for true diversity.

As a PWN Global and Chapter president, I had several conversations with women in companies supposedly focusing on advancing women. When I took a closer look, I saw companies representing only one type of women. This, while stating they are diversity experts, claiming the D&I space. We want leadership to represent diversity but accept that D&I experts represent just one part of the scale.

The message to men and women is not to call yourself diverse and inclusive just because you checked the gender box. How inclusive are you regarding other ethnicities, skin colors, and cultural backgrounds, across and within your gender?

I always believed, as a person of color, that hard work and integrity would take me to the top. We all know this is part of the strategy. Thanks to the leadership in companies I've worked for, I have received the opportunity to step up into new roles. But it is not a given, and I feel I have to work even harder to receive the same acknowledgement as my white, male peers.

So yes, it is possible. And I choose to believe that most people in leadership positions are willing to welcome women and women of color, into the leadership ranks of their organizations.

However, reality shows us that we need to look at why women, women of color, and other minorities are not well represented in corporate leadership.

Recruiting women

Before an organization can even start promoting women into leadership roles, they need to recruit the women who are starting their careers. They also need to recruit women who are ready to take on strategic leadership roles. The latter is often the issue. Aside from the argument, 'we can't find them', hiring women in strategic roles is often seen as risky business. Management, when hiring strategic leadership, requires trust. They need the ability to separate the professional capabilities and experiences, from the diversity ambition.

Hiring a woman is often seen as a way to comply with gender equality demands. When a woman is hired, and she fails, the result is that traditional leadership falls back to 'proven' practices of hiring. In other words, hire what we know. Imagine hiring a woman of color in a strategic role within, for example, a tech company run by 'default men'. The higher the ranks in the company, the more leadership should be able to separate the professionalism and competences, with the focus on gender.

In my experience, keeping women in the organization is the actual bottleneck. Hiring women is the easiest part. And quotas made us focus on hitting diversity numbers. But if you need to keep the focus on attracting women into your company, it means that women are leaving at the same speed. The reason for this is that (traditional) leadership is often not equipped or ready to lead diverse teams. Adding diversity to your team means a diversified leadership style. This is, in most companies, not a part of the management curriculum or KPI's. Aside from gender, being able to lead different people and intersectionality is crucial for the organization to reap the benefits of diverse teams.

Diversity in technology

During my graduation over 20 years ago, women were scarce. To be precise, I was one of the two women who graduated from my school. I started my career in IT and worked in different functions like tech consultant, architecture, sales, and management consultant. The environment I worked in was quite challenging, from a cultural point of view. Women were a minority and the majority worked in staff functions. Also, India wasn't yet a big tech resource country, so my colleagues were all, without exception, white men.

The company's leadership was traditional and not used to working with women, let alone diversity in general. This was hard, especially after a couple of years, when my development showed the need for promotions and the glass ceiling shone brightly.

Nowadays, I work in a leadership role, with HR and P&L responsibility. The step to leadership is made, but the scrutiny remains. Being successful in your job and ticking boxes is essential and part of the job. The challenge for women, and even more for women of color, is balancing to stay true to yourself. This while trying to fit into a culture and comply with leadership styles that is still effective for a less diverse environment. As a single woman in a team, you can easily be pushed into a role like a diversity peacemaker. The 'we need a woman in the team' position is filled. Check the box and carry on This is something that most women accept and decide that it is not an issue for them. The question remains, does this change the culture and stimulate diversity and inclusion?

A word of advice

If you are a woman of any color, or part of the LBTQ community, or not a 'default' man[1], realize that diversity and inclusivity starts with you. We all have biases, and we all make assumptions. Until recently within PWN, many city networks did not allow men in their membership base, let alone in their leadership ranks, which is odd. PWN strives for gender-balanced leadership.

Also, can you look at your environment without any biases? Biases inherited from your parents or social circles? Do you make judgements without seeing color or making assumptions about levels of professionalism? Most of us would say: 'of course I can'. You might even say 'I do not see color'.

Being a woman of color, I always thought I was color blind and treated everyone equally. Learning more and more about biases, I realize that my biases raise their ugly heads when I am not expecting them. Introspection and self-reflection are crucial.

A Call to Action!

If you are working in a (tech) company or pursuing a strategic role in a company that is not working towards D&I, find your allies. Find a sponsor and a mentor in the company who can help you navigate challenges. Also, share your experiences with trusted advisors or a coach, who can help you strategize your career path and deal with difficult situations. When you work for a longer time in a certain environment, you lose your curiosity. You might even tolerate certain questionable behaviors.

We are witnessing a significant change in our society. The role of men and women in business and society is changing. Traditional functions and patterns will vanish, and the next generations will face different challenges that need diversity of thought, skills, and experiences. We all have a role to play in this crucial transition. Be part of this change.

Footnotes

[1] "The default men" is a phrase I borrowed from Jeff Turner, VP of Sustainability at DSM.

21 Francia Agterhof

Francia Agterhof *believes in the power of combining the unique strengths of people working towards a common goal. As a Team Talent Coach, she helps entrepreneurs and small business owners to recognize and use the talents of themselves and of their team. This guarantees the most powerful and meaningful results. It's easier to improve your performance from an 8 to a 9 than from a 3 to 4.*

Francia studied public administration at the University of Twente. She worked in both the public and private sectors, and coaches for almost two decades now.

To contact Francia: linkedin.com/in/franciaagterhof
→ *talententaal.nl*

The Power of Mutual, Talent Based Growth

Having a coach nowadays is popular among people who want to grow. You might think that in a coaching relationship only the coachee grows. But that is far from the reality. One of the most beautiful gifts from the coaching relationship is the bilateral growth that happens. I want to share with you my journey of collective success.

My first job was in a financial environment. After a year, I discovered that numbers didn't interest me enough; certainly not for 40 hours a week. I decided to switch careers, to do what I had always wanted to do.

In 2000, I began my coaching education. Even 20 years later, I still remember the voice of my teacher and coach Marijke Lingsma. I can feel the atmosphere of the hotel and see the dust of the conference chair. Feeling tired, overwhelmed, practicing again and again with finding the right questions. I hear her voice; she always spoke softly. I carry a sentence she used with me. Over the years, I translated it into my own words: 'If you are coaching, you have to be in development.' Because the person you coach also brings something to you. You cannot help them if you are not also developing. Continuing growth has become a habit of mine.

Here I share with you three professional experiences that I cherish. They all had a great impact on my life. You will meet Kanako, who travelled a long road and succeeded; Miro, who recognized his talents and started his own business; and Grazia, with whom I collaborate to give workshops to the owners of small and mid-sized businesses, to empower them and help them perform better.

Kanako

Persevering even when things get tough

In 2011, our family moved from The Hague to Eindhoven in the Netherlands, due to a change in my husband's job. I had to quit my job helping non-native mothers of primary school children with the Dutch language. I helped them practice writing, reading, listening, and speaking, so they could communicate in Dutch with their children, as well as with the teachers, or the doctor, etc.

In Eindhoven, outside the school our children attended, I met Kanako, a smart, highly educated foreign psychologist. She told me she was currently learning Dutch. I recognized some of her difficulties with Dutch while she was speaking to me. She wanted to use her education and 15 years of experience from her home country, here in the Netherlands. However, she was having trouble being understood by new potential employers. She felt angry and misunderstood; getting rejected, hearing over and over again, that what she wanted to achieve was not possible.

Kanako needed someone to listen to her and help her find her way in the Dutch culture. I was willing to use my experience and started to give her Dutch conversation lessons. Also, I have always enjoyed working with highly educated people. I decided to accompany Kanako on her path to reach her goal; a path that took several years.

We started off by composing a document to show what she had done in the 15 years of her working life. I was impressed.

She focused on improving her Dutch communication skills, going from beginner to intermediate, to a professional working level. She found an internship that helped her get the necessary work experience. Every step she took helped her get closer to accreditation as a psychologist. After five years, she succeeded.

What I learned from her is to persevere. I must admit, I sometimes had my doubts. There are so many psychologists in the Netherlands and meeting all the requirements takes such a long time. Kanako was also the first person with her nationality who took this path. I often questioned if this would work out in the end. I couldn't imagine myself walking this long path to be recognized for my skills and experience in a foreign country.

It did work out and it changed my thinking. Nowadays, she works as a registered psychologist. She kept going after what she wanted. Now, whenever I think a task is difficult to accomplish, I look to her as my role model. She taught me to follow my path and do what it takes. It took almost five years, but she proved it was doable. It's a message I pass on to entrepreneurs: don't give up! Even if the path feels long, you will get there in the end.

Miro

Recognizing our talents

From 2011 to 2016, besides giving conversation lessons, I also followed all kinds of courses about finance, personal development, and business/entrepreneurship. I wanted to learn and to develop. My first introduction to Miro was during that period. Every Tuesday, I received a new blog post from the Open Circles Academy, at that time the most active blog for entrepreneurs in the Netherlands. The blogs were inspiring, full of energy and very relatable. I recognized myself when I was reading the blogs. Miro translated and ghostwrote those blogs.

So, when I got the opportunity to follow a free workshop he was giving, I went. I will never forget this moment. I wanted to learn how to write like him, so I could inspire and give value to my coachees through my own blog. Miro took out a blank sheet of paper and started asking questions, brainstorming, and writing down whatever came into his mind. This was his way to collect topics to write about. His creativity and his brainstorming method opened doors for me. I could see his experience and his expertise. It all looked so easy when he showed it to me. I was flabbergasted because I knew at that moment, I couldn't do what he was doing.

In 2016, I met Miro again during an event. I shared with him the experience I had during his workshop and asked why he didn't start for himself? We helped each other: he with a quick scan of my business and me with recognizing his talents. Two years later, Miro contacted me to thank me for this moment because it helped him to start for himself. He became conscious of his possibilities.

Miro taught me that we tend to take our own talents for granted. What we do is easy to us and we assume it's easy for others as well. We often need other people to recognize our skills. He recognized the coach in me, just as I recognized his writing talent. As soon as you become aware of your talents, your energy starts flowing. It makes it so much easier to follow your path. Don't underestimate yourself!

Grazia

Collaborating to make the most of complementary talents

After my experience with Miro, I continued to develop talent management for small and mid-sized businesses and entrepreneurs. I am convinced that everyone has 5 top talents. My goal is to help entrepreneurs recognize these talents.

My third learning experience was with Grazia. We also met each other through Open Circles. Grazia and I shared our experiences and started to meet regularly. In 2017, we began working together and we still do. She is great with numbers and loves to collect the right information in the form of data and facts. From all the available information, she is able to select the most important facts. And with this data, she bases her decisions which helps the organization with their finances.

When I see her working, it looks so simple. I really admire her skill with numbers.

During our collaboration, I discovered how Grazia helps me with my talent in a way that continuously produces new ideas. In the beginning, there are only vague ideas, like during a brainstorming. Then Grazia starts to question me, using one of her talents, because she needs something more tangible than just an idea. Thanks to her questions, my idea starts to get more concrete. She helps me to translate the idea into a practical application.

From Grazia, I learned the great experience of how to complement each other's talents. We have different talents, thoughts, and feelings. As well, we are different in how we act. We learned to recognize and appreciate the differences between us. And like the above example, we learned to make use of our differences in a productive and energizing way.

Continuing to collaborate, we discovered how we could pool our experiences and help mid-sized businesses and entrepreneurs. We collaborate with both the strategical financial goals and numbers, combined with the individual talents of the people. This provides the energy to reach those goals.

How can talents help you?

What helps you to persevere and do what you have to do? We saw the journeys of collective success. All of the encounters I've described are about growth: the growth of Kanako, Miro, and Grazia but also mine.

Kanako and unconscious talents

In the example of Kanako, we weren't aware of our talents. We just acted naturally but at the same time unconsciously used our talents. Her work today as a registered psychologist in the Netherlands, after several years of frustration, is a perfect example. Working with Kanako unlocked my talent.

This example shows you that talents work unconsciously. You can recognize them if you ask yourself to identify a moment you are proud of, which went really well. Make that very specific: what action did you take? In which situation? Who was with you?

<u>Miro recognizing talent</u>
In the example of Miro, I saw him doing his job as a translator and ghostwriter very naturally. I signaled how easy it was for him. I complimented him on this. My simple observation about this talent inspired him to start his own business.

You can recognize these talents by asking yourself: what do I do easily? When do I get compliments? Again, make those questions very specific.

<u>Grazia and Collaboration</u>
In my experience with Grazia, we were conscious that our talents complemented each other perfectly.

How can you use your talents to reach your goal together with a partner, so that your talents complement each other?

A Call to Action!

All my examples show one thing: everyone has their own talents, everyone! It is great to see your talents working when you use them and just as great to see them developing. What is even nicer is when you work together, growth is accelerated. As a coach, you have the privilege to help people growing. In that growth, you also grow yourself. Like one of my coaching teachers told me: 'as a coach you need to be in development'. We saw that working for Kanako, Miro, and Grazia. How about you? How are you developing?

22 Shokoofeh Ketabchi

***Dr. Shokoofeh Ketabchi PhD** is a highly educated businesswoman, entrepreneur, and author. She has worked in several industries and countries as a business consultant, helping companies to improve their performance and expand to new markets. Having a busy lifestyle and always traveling made it difficult for her to stay healthy and fit. So, she developed a program called Tanfit. This helps people with a busy lifestyle, like her, to be able to exercise and stay fit and healthy whenever and wherever they are.*

She currently resides in Amsterdam and enjoys the multicultural and diverse atmosphere of the city. Her main hobbies are reading books and playing tennis. She is hardworking, self-motivated, energetic, and hopes to change the world for the better!

→ *To contact Shokoofeh: linkedin.com/in/dr-shokoofeh-ketabchi*
tanfit.shop

Women's Relationship with Power

It is an amazing time to be a woman! We have never been as powerful and determined as we are now. We form half the labor force[1] and hold strategic positions in many countries around the globe. The world is moving towards a more feminine type of leadership with regards to communities, societies, and organizations. There have been so many well-known role models and celebrated world leaders, like Jacinda Ardern, who serves as the 40th prime minister of New Zealand.

Moreover, women's collective efforts all around the world have led to developing shelters, schools, hospitals, libraries, and many more facilities which help to improve and enhance their communities. They are the primary caretakers and educators of the family and are global volunteers when a disaster strikes.

However, when it comes to advocating power, we approach it with loads of insecurities and uncertainties. We are afraid to be punished or isolated by the society which calls powerful women various unfair names. As well, the political climate is not in favor of women: there are still major topics, such as gender pay gaps and human rights issues, in many parts of the world. Nevertheless, we can take some initiatives to overcome these issues and fix our relationship with power. In this essay, I will provide some practical steps to overcome our self-doubt and take charge!

Finding your voice

Sheryl Sandburg serves as the Chief Operating Officer of Facebook and is the founder of LeanIn.org. She has helped many women throughout the years, to bring the limitations and obstacles residing within themselves under control. Sheryl, now a successful business executive, used to downplay her power and success out of fear of paying a penalty for being popular.

In her successful bestselling book, 'Lean In', she mentions how finding her voice helped her to gain control over her insecurities and pursue her ambitions further. She explicitly encourages women to follow their dreams, while getting the most support that they can. One of the major points she emphasizes, is to make your spouse your 'truly equal partner' at home; to create an optimum family/work-life relationship for both.

In addition, finding our voice helps us to shift from outdated and oppressive behavior to an unequivocal transformation of how we live and work. We need to transform our own relationship with power. Many of us think power is violent, unfeminine, dominant, and intrusive. All these types of associations with power are oppressive, old-fashioned, and patriarchal. Always ask yourself this question: would men think power is violent and intrusive? If your answer is 'no', you have to rethink and be more critical with your own beliefs and change your attitude and behavior accordingly.

Find your voice and pursue your dreams and ambitions. Being ambitious is aspirational and empowering. It is having a goal, hope, and desire, while working hard towards it. Ambition leads to being able to take responsibility and stand by your goals and opinions. It changes our behavior: from being reactive to the opinion or decision of others about us, to becoming proactive. We need to lead based upon our own decisions and opinions.

Define your own terms

Finding your voice entails taking charge of your own decisions; and now is the time to define your own terms. If you do not define them for yourself, someone else will and then you have to follow. Be determined and intentional. Set your goals with confidence and strength to define the direction of how things are supposed to happen. In addition, you need to become fluent in the language of power. In other words, you need to learn what power means in different people's views, genders, and cultures. You need to be able to communicate successfully across teams and people, while holding onto your terms and values.

We need to be starters. When we start, we set the tone for the rest of the campaign, conversation, or even the direction of the business. Let us start by setting the first steps and guiding the rest. At the same time, we have to be good finishers and have the last word. Women have to sit at the table, start the conversation, and stay engaged until the end. That is the only way we can make everyone aware of our terms and set the pace for the rest of the journey.

On the other hand, when women define their own terms, they will be taken seriously and gain more credibility. This will help them to be considered for promotion and future career opportunities which come along the way. For this purpose, we need to master various communication behaviors and attitudes to strengthen our impact and credibility at work. These behaviors include managing interruptions and 'taking back the floor', when it happens, at meetings or gatherings by colleagues. The result will show you are in control and consequently gives you more credibility.

Put your feminine power into action

The image of power and leadership has been portrayed as masculine, linear, decisive, goal oriented, and individualistic (independent and self-reliant). However, the world is moving toward a more collective attitude, in which the skills mentioned above could be necessary but not enough. Therefore, characteristics like inclusion, empathy, finding common ground, collective intelligence, compassion, and building bridges are increasingly emphasized and required in the world.

These feminine characteristics are not limited to women. Yet, the media criticizes or completely ignores such feminine skills. As a result, we need to stay strong and believe in the power of our innate skills. The current situation and especially the changes we went through in 2020, requires a more compassionate and sympathetic approach in the workspace and ultimately, to leadership.

Moreover, we have clearly seen that women-led countries have performed much better during the pandemic in 2020. According to an article published in the UK Guardian, research demonstrates that women-led countries started the lockdown much earlier and suffered half as many deaths on average as those led by men. "The relative early success of leaders such as Germany's Angela Merkel, New Zealand's Jacinda Ardern, Denmark's Mette Frederiksen, Taiwan's Tsai Ing-wen and Finland's Sanna Marin has so far attracted many headlines but little academic attention."[2]

The analysis of the results clearly demonstrated that being proactive and compassionate, while implementing coordinated and collective policy responses, were among the skills applied by women leaders achieving amazing results. So, embrace your feminine power and let it shine through. Lighten up the world that needs it now, more than ever.

Connect and empower your network

As women move forward in the power structures of economic and political institutions, we face cultural and systemic obstacles that evidently make it difficult to progress further. One way to overcome this issue is to keep a close circle of connections and share our experiences to help and learn from each other. After we get help, have overcome the obstacles, and moved forward, it is our turn to look around and reach out to other women and lift them up. In fact, as we grow, we have access to more critical information and resources. Why not share these with other women and support them in acquiring and utilizing the necessary skills. They too advance and benefit us, as well as everyone else, in return.

Many women underestimate the power of networking. We need to prioritize building relationships. We do not work with companies; we work with people who do business with those whom they like and trust. Therefore, it is important to create meaningful relationships and support and mentor each other. Women can create a much bigger impact and change in the world when they are part of a community and a larger network.

A Call to Action!

By finding our voices, defining our own terms and credibility, and claiming our feminine power, we will grow in energy and purpose to create a better world that benefits everyone. Therefore, it is time to support each other, to connect, and exchange ideas. No one is as creative and powerful individually, as we can be together.

Above all, I cannot emphasize enough the great advantage of being part of a community of women, with whom we share information and ideas to help each other to grow. I once read this next sentence somewhere and it has stayed with me ever since: 'a woman alone has power, but collectively we can have an impact'. So, let us be part of a greater impact.

Finally, I have always been asked:

- How do we find our network of women?
- Who do we socialize with to benefit each other?

The answer is to search for people whom you admire, contact them, and ask for advice and their feedback. Then follow up and stay in touch. If there is a bigger network, make sure to create a relationship with all those who you admire, following the previously mentioned principles. In addition, I recommend to always participate, always be present, and make your presence known to the community. Networks naturally cannot count much on the passive members, so be active, shine and make a difference!

Footnotes

[1] worldbank.org

[2] theguardian.com/world/2020/aug/18/female-led-countries-handled-coronavirus-better-study-jacinda-ardern-angela-merkel

23

Albane Houri

Albane Houri *is a French national with over 20 years of international experience in the corporate finance and accounting field.*

She has been living in the United States, France, and Switzerland before moving in 2017 to Amsterdam, the Netherlands. She has worked for diverse businesses with very different cultures: French TV, American Industrial large and less large corporations with diverse degree of internationalization of the management team.

Even though Albane's career is focused on finance and accounting activities, the purpose of the company she is working for has been taking an increasing importance to her over the past 10 years. She is now working in the food/ life sciences industry where technology developments are growing alternative proteins options. This is making the public desire for a healthier and more environmentally conscious food possible.

In her free time, Albane enjoys working out, exchanging with the international community, listening and dancing to live music, and travelling independently.

→ *To contact Albane: linkedin.com/in/albanehouri-executivemba/*

A Confused State of Affairs

I have always been fascinated by human interactions. In this essay, I focus on how people react as a consequence of their education and their environment. So, what could be better topics to discuss than diversity, inclusion, and the gender gap?

I grew up in a family where the older generation was quite old fashioned in dealing with gender. My origins are mixed between South and Eastern Europe, and Middle East North Africa. I was lucky to be educated in a high school where there were a lot of foreigners. This diversity of origins, experiences, and references was something I always enjoyed.

In my childhood, my first best friend was a boy. I have always played with my male cousins and my male friends as if there was no gender difference. Running as quick or even quicker than the boys, I was completely accepted in their group, or at least that was the feeling I had. Later, I went to a girls-only private Catholic school. The life objective for many of my classmates was to marry a wealthy, charismatic, and successful man, have children, and be a housewife. The lack of variety in the potential future they were imagining for themselves saddened me. I didn't feel able to convince them that there were other options. What did I really know about what would make them happy?

Starting my professional life in the financial world, I was quite confused in what to expect from men and women. What I lacked was a role model, as well as the knowledge, in dealing equally with the other gender, as my new experiences were often disappointing.

Who of us has not felt this discrepancy in a professional setting? It was recognizable when I realized I was being assessed differently by men in positions not necessarily more senior than I was; they only saw me as a woman, when all I really wanted is for them to see me as a smart colleague!

Too many times in my life I felt overwhelmed by the looks on their faces. Obviously, they weren't focusing on my professional qualifications. Added to this mix was the jealously some women exhibited, viewing me as a strong competitor. What I was looking for were supportive professional relationships, and possibly to make friends! It was, I suppose, a somewhat natural reaction. We worked in an environment which didn't provide many opportunities for women advancing their careers.

Let me give you an example of the first situation. My name is not very common. People from other countries can't always assign a gender to my given name. This means, before I enter a room of strangers, they don't know if I'm a man or a woman before they meet me. More than 10 years ago, I was invited to a meeting, in my new role as the Finance Lead for a manufacturing facility located outside of Paris. It was a few weeks after starting in this position, in a newly formed business unit. People didn't know me. The meeting was taking place in person, in the south of the Netherlands.

I entered the room and started introducing myself. About 90% of the men in the room looked in astonishment at me. Some of them even commented about being astounded that Albane Houri, in a manufacturing finance position, was actually a woman. Why were they so sure it was a man taking on this job position? It actually made me smile. I do like to surprise people.

With experience, I learned to view their reactions as a way for them to show dominance; a kind of required reaction, though not a fair one. It took me many years to feel confident when these kinds of situations occur. That being said, there is still room in my professional life for improvement in how I handle them. These experiences have taught me to recognize and appreciate my allies.

To me, the toughest hurdle in the gender gap is the support that men give each other; the atmosphere of brotherhood they create. In my experience, women are not inclined to do the same in sisterhood.

I see some of my male colleagues bonding closely together because they face the same challenges in their personal life, often putting their jobs before their families. They are helping each other to not feel guilty about the choices they're making. Why wouldn't they naturally choose to be more supportive of one of their brothers, when there are discussions about a promotion?

Women can be so much tougher on each other, while I see men as more forgiving towards each other. It especially saddens me seeing women, in an attempt to being more accepted in this male 'club', willing to belittle other women. This has unsettled me several times, when I've been on the receiving end in these situations. In my eyes, this kind of behavior goes against common decency, and is a totally unprincipled strategy. It is also such an energy drainer for both sides.

There is truly a disconnect between what I see happening and what I feel deep inside as being right and ethical. It has always made me so uncomfortable. The key is to keep on following our values, stand up, say no or stop when we know something is wrong. We need to use the power we inherently have, keeping our values well in sight, and never crossing the line. The reality is, we women are so much stronger, if only we would recognize it.

There are, however, men and women who see women for their full potential; combining brain power with charm to make their business impact even stronger. They see us as a great asset. When they do, we succeed in building powerful teams together. When we bring different backgrounds and perspectives to the team, we are naturally developing better solutions. Teamwork is made so much more efficient and effective, when everyone is listening to each other; when we are making sure that the voice of each of our teammates is heard and their inputs are valued, with no one trying to dominate.

I have been happily surprised this past year with the group work done in the Executive MBA, which I recently finished. Even though it's not real life or without the financial impact from the decisions made, I felt the effects of successful collaborations. Working in groups, with members coming from different backgrounds, including business owners, I found myself positively surprised. I had expected to face many of the common stereotypes, such as men who are used to being in a decision-making position. But actually, I didn't experience much of these stereotypes. I found open-minded men, ready to listen to the inputs of the women, and ready to value us equally and objectively.

To the younger generation, I want to tell you to be strong and trust in yourself; more than I did when I was younger. I wish for you to hear less that women are all about feelings, implying that our decisions need to be challenged. So many decisions I made were based on facts. Now I am at a point in my life where I am going to start thinking and acting differently. I'll consider my feelings and my well-being as more central in my decision-making process.

It makes me smile to think that I will be going forward, acting exactly like the stereotypical expectations of a woman. I will stand by my choices, be more in harmony with what can make me be happy, and let go of what people think.

A Call to Action!

Be well-grounded in life and believe that dreams can be reached. It's just a matter of leveraging natural talents and working hard when things don't come naturally.

Hold your head up, look proudly and fiercely to the future ahead of you. Don't mind the unprofessional stares and behaviors. Just keep on looking straight ahead and smile! Find your allies and forget about what the others think or how they act. They might change their mind eventually. Much of changing mindset is about education. Some people can get out of the grey zone and into the light, at some point in their life.

Take time to look back at all the fights you've already won and the ones you didn't. Learn from your mistakes and get stronger as the securely vulnerable woman you are. Know yourself! Know what you want to attain, what the compromises are that you are willing to make and the ones that you're not. Because at the end of the day, what really counts is that you are happy and well-rooted in your life, supported equally by men and women.

24

Mark Cavallo

***Mark Cavallo** is a holistic leadership coach specializing in self-awareness and emotional fitness. He is passionate about enriching people's lives through deep coaching, in merging the logical, rational intellect with the powerful, underlying emotions that together form our beliefs, motivations, behaviors, and patterns. He is stoked to be able to contribute to a book that genuinely aims to promote gender equality and diversity within leadership globally. It's a movement that needs the cooperation and collaboration of everyone, if it is to achieve its goals.*

This book, Ready For Female Leadership, is a heartfelt, passionate call to arms for everyone, everywhere, to become more conscious of the underlying inequalities in our lives and how we can individually add to the collective effort to redress the lack of balance.

Men, it's time to step up to the challenge and contribute to the empowerment of women in leadership roles!

→ *To contact Mark: linkedin.com/in/markcavallo-coaching*
markcavallocoaching.com

Why Empathetic, Compassionate Men Need to Step Up

My daughter's birth in 2007 was a peak experience for me, for more than the obvious reason. Gay men with children were a relatively rare phenomenon back then (although unsolicited advice and judgement around the event wasn't). I had asked Milla's future mother to co-parent with me, with the understanding that I would be sharing the joy, burden, challenges, and responsibility of raising our child. But more than that, becoming a father to a daughter offered me a unique and golden opening into the (hitherto) mysterious world of women's emotions, hormones, operating systems, and their unique talents. For the first time perhaps, I started becoming aware of, and interested in, the puzzling prejudice, clichés, and metaphorical barriers that have historically been placed on their path.

During her young life, Milla and I have experienced our fair share of hardship. At age 10, she had a brain hemorrhage which left its mark physically on her and emotionally on all of us. We suddenly found ourselves intensely supporting our daughter through a traumatic life and (potential) death experience, which had no precedent. A situation which I was particularly unprepared for emotionally. This harrowing experience, coupled with my own struggles of growing up in a poor, hetero-normative environment of immigrant parents and the ensuing years of bullying, offered hidden gifts that changed my life path.

I have come to view these gifts as sisters: interwoven and of blood decent; related and interdependent, yet separate.

Empathy and compassion

Why is it more vital now, than ever before, to continue to highlight, table, discuss, and action the discrepancies between women and men in the workplace? Because a lack of workplace diversity and in this case, gender inequality, are massive barriers. They are robbing the world of different perspectives, skills, innate characteristics, and solutions. The fact that women are (variable according to region of course) still denied equitable access to work and study opportunities, to promotion and advancement, senior positions, and government roles, is inexcusable. Especially in the west.

In a world largely formed and run by men, women have been battling to find a footing on territory they had little say in molding. Battling for rights and opportunities they've traditionally been denied, whilst carrying on their 'motherhood duties'. If we look at the domain of work, progress has been made but it is still surprisingly persistent.

When you look at the statistics, they are disheartening. The glass ceiling continues to be made of crack-resistant material. According to the UN, between 1995 and 2019:

- women's representation in senior executive positions remained stable at around 28%
- female vs male labor participation gap remained around 25% in favor of men
- 7,4% of Fortune 500 CEOs were female (the New York Times wrote in 2015 that there were more CEOs named John than there were female CEOs)
- 18% of generally surveyed companies had female CEOs

Women have been more successful in penetrating into government leadership roles, but even so, at 22% they remain underrepresented. I find that astounding. Especially when I consider that an S&P Global Market Intelligence report from 2019 states: "Female CEOs drove more value appreciation and improved stock price momentum for their firms, and female CFOs drove more value appreciation, better defended profitability moats, and delivered excess risk-adjusted returns for their firms."

It's clear that us men rule the world and set the general values, expectations, belief systems, roles, and laws that work to protect our position. So, how do we go about bringing balance to a system inherently resistant to it?

The answer is: empathy and compassion.

A quick recap. Empathy is defined in a multitude of ways. Here are two of them:
Cognitive empathy: the ability to imagine what someone else may be thinking or feeling. It's basically an intellectual approach of trying to recreate in your head what the other person may be thinking or feeling.

Emotional empathy: being able to 'walk in someone else's shoes to feel what they are feeling'. It's a more visceral empathy, as it really reproduces a physiological response in your body that mirrors that of someone else's. My daughter taught me much about this particular type of empathy. Being able to open up, hold space for her, and support her in her grief, has transformed our relationship and added a string to my empathy bow.

Compassion: my core value. It's the secret superpower that can change the world. Not only can we empathize / feel along with someone, but we also want to alleviate their suffering, improve their life, and be with them. A practical, other-directed, love-fueled connecting action that fuses the us / them divide and helps us to focus on what makes us similar.

The funny thing about empathy is that it can sometimes conflict with that moral value we vaguely call justice. In a series of experiments, conducted in 2016 for the Journal of Personality and Social Psychology, participants were found to act preferentially in favor of an individual, but against the principle of justice, if they were induced to feel empathy for them. However, if they didn't feel empathy for the participants, they acted in accordance with the principle of justice when it came to an equitable distribution of resources.

So, how can empathy and compassion, which according to research are skills inherently more present in women, be leveraged and deployed effectively to promote the well-being, equality, and inclusion of women in a male-dominated world?

If you apply the implications to advancing gender equality at work, we are presented with a dichotomy of sorts. If we favor those with whom we empathize the most, at the cost of a sense of justice, then what are the repercussions for women with respect to equitable division of opportunities and advancement? How can they gain access to resources when, men are far and away the decision makers?

Fortunately, empathy is a skill that can be learned. What's interesting to me is that when I run workshops for corporations on the topic of empathy, women connect to emotional empathy, whereas men can relate to cognitive empathy. Emotional equals experiencing the feelings; cognitive equals thinking what they may be feeling or thinking. Cognitive is also known as perspective taking.

So how can us males consciously contribute to the continuing, accelerating equality and diversity in the workforce, in particular with respect to women? There's obviously not one answer to this. Below are some ideas that leaders, managers, CEOs, employees, start-ups, gen X Y Z, and boomers can all apply, if they wish to do so.

Close the gender empathy gap.

Generally speaking, men are attracted to monetary rewards, while women are attracted more to work flexibility and adaptable conditions. Given the dominance of men in leadership positions, what can we do to understand this gap and take steps to close it?

1. Ask for employee feedback on the issue and be prepared to act on it.

2. Approach issues with your heart and head.
3. Get help from a coach, therapist, etc., if needed.
4. Literally walk in someone else's shoes, whether by volunteering, participating in a work sponsored program along those lines, or in your private life.
5. Clarify your own biases: conscious and subconscious!
6. Be curious: approach others and issues with curiosity, an open heart and mind.
7. Learn to ask better questions.

Cultivate personal empathy

1. Practice active listening: show an interest in what is being said and in who is saying it. Avoid advice, opinions, and hijacking the content.
2. Imagine when you see or read about someone who has experienced 'trauma' or difficult circumstances, what they may have been feeling, what they may have been thinking.
3. Imagine a person, with whom you have trouble empathizing, as a young girl or boy; picture them at age 6 or 10. How do you feel about them now? Where is that person now? Focus on what the motivation could be for their behavior (pain, frustration, fear, etc.) and show empathy with them.
4. Focus on what unites us: our similarities and struggles, our common interests, and the need to be seen, heard, and understood.
5. SPEAK UP! When a situation arises in which women are disadvantaged (and there are many biases around pay, performance, and promotion), make it a point to open up the debate and action it to resolve the differences.

But the most important way to continue working on reducing any gap, real and perceived, between people at work, is to get men involved in the conversation, and to get men removed from the conversation (only partly kidding).

So, men, the time for the patriarchal society has come and gone. We wouldn't work for less money for similar jobs. We wouldn't tolerate being interrupted constantly during meetings (research shows men interrupt women twice as much as women interrupt men). We wouldn't tolerate being told by women how and what we may or may not do with our bodies.

When I think of my daughter and her physical challenges, I'm even more grateful that we have spent her whole life championing her, encouraging her to raise her voice. To ask for what she needs and to have an awareness that we are all worthy humans; worthy of love, respect, and achieving our dreams. I'm an example for her of how men and women can relate to each other (and any other human being, whether they identify with the woman/man label or not). My values will be absorbed to an extent by her, and her expectations will be formed by them.

A Call to Action!

Men need to set the example for other men of what gender equality looks like. Simply be empathetic: imagine what it would be like to be underpaid, underappreciated, and generally viewed as being 'weaker'. This can spark the start of a process that leads to action; to wanting to elevate each other, bring fairness and equality into play without the outdated and irrelevant notion of men versus women or any other gender identifier.

25 Bernice Feller-Thijm

Bernice Feller-Thijm *is an Inclusion Strategist & Team Performance Coach, who for over 20 years, has led and facilitated teams. According to her, differences, resistance, and complexity are not obstacles, but rather the fuel for sustainable change.*

With her company, JustB, Bernice facilitates sessions in which strategy and policy related to diversity and inclusion are translated into concrete action. For this she uses systems theory, which is based on the question 'what is needed to make the entire system better'. She helps teams create a space with psychological safety in which all colleagues can communicate constructively and connect authentically.

→ *To contact Bernice: linkedin.com/in/bernicethijm/*
justb.agency/

Genuine Connections: establishing inclusive work and life spaces

One of the things I enjoy most in life is spending time with friends, family, and loved ones. But also with people I might not know very well. Talking, listening, learning, and laughing. That interaction, being part of the same bubble for a little while, is sometimes all you need to lift yourself up when you need it most. Leaving an encounter enriched, smarter, or happier because you experienced that genuine, human connection. The value of this has become even more apparent since COVID-19 changed our lives and impacted how we can interact with each other on a daily basis. I think it is fascinating how we are asked to adapt and find new ways to sustain genuine connections. How do we manage to stay connected?

Creating genuine connections

My curiosity about making connections was the reason and motivation I got onto the internet in 2000. The ability to create instant connections all over the world was truly powerful. I started working in start-ups, and later on in corporates, creating digital strategies on how best to make connections through digital channels. By 2012, the internet had evolved considerably, and I started noticing the disconnect that occurred online. Noticing the difference between connecting and making a genuine connection, I started to miss the genuine person to person connection. The things people put online increasingly became less about who they really are. We make avatar to avatar connections and not a human-to-human connection. Once I realized this, I decided to step back, to be more offline, and to reinvestigate what it means to create that genuine connection. And this time, with the added objective to generate these connections to facilitate systemic and sustainable change within organizations. And if I dare to be really ambitious, the world. That is the reason I now work as an inclusion strategist and team performance coach.

I firmly believe that if we are to solve today's complex problems, achieve better business results, and create social equity, we must involve everyone. This requires an ability to combine different perspectives, to make room for uniqueness, and to unlock full potential.

Diversity, Equity and Inclusion

We need diversity of thought and perspectives to achieve meaningful impact. And at its core, it starts with genuine connection. And this is what I'm about. Passionate about DEI: Diversity, Equity, and Inclusion. I feel the latter is what is truly needed, in order to create a world wherein we all feel we're part of it: we're valued, feel we belong, and have equity in opportunity, so we can participate.

Without inclusiveness, no-one can uniquely manifest what they are passionate about. This is what I aim to enable in organizations. Creating inclusive cultures, wherein people are able to express their 'unique U' as a person. To be able to voice their unique perspective. Diversity is about manifesting what is unique about each of us. This takes work on the part of the group but also of the individual: confronting limiting beliefs, being courageous, and speaking up, asking the questions which need to be asked, and having the bold conversations which need to be had.

Emotional Intelligence

This is where emotional intelligence plays a big role. We know that emotional intelligence (EI) is linked to fostering creative and inclusive cultures. The definition I use of EI[1] is the ability to recognize and be able to correctly label emotions in ourselves, as well as in others. This EI is then used to guide one's thinking, change behavior, adjust emotions, and adapt to different environments in order to achieve one's goals.

In order to hone one's EI, there are a set of personal qualities or characteristics which can and need to be developed. They will ensure DEI becomes part of our personal and professional DNA.
I believe the foundation of EI rests on greater self-awareness or self-knowledge. People with a developed EI can register having an emotion by being aware of what signals they're experiencing. They can discern what kind of emotion they're having. They do this by stopping to check in with themselves and question the thoughts or feelings they're experiencing. Reflecting and asking if this thought or feeling is serving them, is part of this skill.

In this way, emotional self-regulation is developed, which is the second skill I feel is essential in creating a positive DEI culture. Why? Because it means they're far less likely to be hijacked by their emotions. Courageous conversations are needed to achieve results, and emotionally aware people are able to handle these in a constructive manner. They're able to reflect and deal with the awkwardness. The pre-frontal cortex, where our creative, logical thinking takes place, is going to be working optimally for and not against them. They're able to make better choices for themselves. If this part of the brain is handicapped by a strong emotion, they're not going to be able to express themselves, to achieve a positive outcome.

By recognizing emotions in others, compassion develops, which is another important skill to operate in inclusive environments. Other characteristics which stand people well with a high level of EI are optimism, motivation, and perseverance.

Unconscious bias

Self-awareness also helps us deal with another big influence on our inclusive behavior: unconscious bias. Largely influenced by the amygdala, it's the part of our primitive brain which kicks in for survival or the fight, flight, freeze response. When a fast car is coming directly towards us, we jump onto the sidewalk to avoid getting run over.

However, this same organ is also responsible for jumping to conclusions. It's filtering, sorting, and comparing millions of signals throughout the day. It's handy since our brain uses this filtering to speed processes along. But it also plays into us having unconscious biases. Therefore, it influences how and why we respond, or why we may or may not connect with others.

Most of us are aware that we have biases. By developing self-awareness, we can stop ourselves, understand, and acknowledge that we're jumping to conclusions. Say, for example, you are reading a resume and you're reaching certain assumptions, based upon your own knowledge and experiences, unrelated to the candidate. Having this ability will make you slow down. You're then able to reset the way you are reading and judging what's actually in that resume.

Another example is having a discussion with a neighbor, and this neighbor looks or sounds like someone from the past, with uncomfortable associations. This subconscious association is going to color your response to your neighbor.

Of course, becoming consciously skilled at all these traits takes time. Are we there yet as a society? The answer is an unequivocal NO. But it is my vision for a sustainable future. Yes, we need to work together as an organization, a team, and as a society. And for DEI to really work, it takes so much commitment on a personal level as well.

I'd like to paint a scenario for you. Let's say we've all moved forward and our workplaces and life spaces are inclusive. It still means that you as an individual need to know what your unique perspective is. How do you put that forward in a confident way? You might have limiting beliefs or have other reasons why you don't feel comfortable speaking up, asking questions, etc. Don't underestimate the role you have to play yourself, to create and reap the benefits of that inclusive workspace or life space you want to make happen.

It's a win-win-win situation

It's truly a win-win-win situation. Society, organizations, and the people working in them, benefit from an inclusive culture in so many ways. Foremost, and most obviously, because it's just the human thing to do. That being said, most organizations are not looking to become a spiritual oasis. But they do want to be successful and profitable. Adapting, staying current, and ahead of your competition are important reasons to invest in DEI. Recognize, incorporate, and utilize all the different perspectives existing within your company.

But remember, it's not just about pulling people together. Look at DEI as a mathematical equation: Innovation = Diversity x Interaction. For really constructive interaction, you need people to feel they are included. A safe psychological environment needs to be created. Employees need to feel they can ask questions, without fear or ridicule. Failure is something to learn from and not to fear. Constructive communication rules. These are the ingredients needed to create the inclusive culture where diversity can flourish. This in turn leads to more creativity, innovation, and sustainable growth.

Making DEI part of our DNA

There are a number of qualities we need to foster in ourselves, in order to make DEI part of our DNA. One is the willingness to learn. The curiosity that comes from being confronted by something unknown or with someone who is so different. This curiosity and willingness to learn colors how one views the world, and how daily life is experienced. This attitude is so valuable to create the environments and cultures we want. Think of everything as opportunities to learn and in that experience, be willing to be vulnerable as well. Be able to say: 'I don't know' or 'I don't understand'. 'Will you help me understand?'. To be compassionate, also towards ourselves. Mistakes will be made on both sides. We won't always know the right thing to say or how to behave. But let's promise each other, 'once we know better, we'll do better', to paraphrase Maya Angelou.

We don't 'unlearn' things quickly. Old habits can die hard. The way our neural circuitry is designed, even though we 'know' something, we won't be able to flawlessly act upon it.

Our innate biases, linked to our primitive survival brain and also to our upbringing, can be weakened. First is to be aware, as I've mentioned earlier. Then take the time to slow down and reflect on what's happened. Is there a thought, experience, or emotion that's causing discomfort? Are there things that can be let go of?

Have the courage to dive into your dark side, when needed. These are things we don't really want to know about ourselves, or don't want to acknowledge about ourselves. Things that make us angry or ashamed. Becoming a friend to our dark side can have so many benefits. By shedding light on these aspects of ourselves, we can begin to change.

There are questions we can ask ourselves or our colleagues, in order to address the underlying feelings or emotions surrounding a topic as sensitive as DEI. I don't think we should aspire to create some sort of list of questions. What we need, is to ensure there is a safe space and a genuine connection with the people around us, to be able to ask these questions. Ask a question in a thoughtful, respectful way. Don't be rushed. Be sincere. Paying attention to the context is perhaps more important than asking the 'right' question. What is the intention in asking this question? By ensuring these guidelines are met and having invested in creating that genuine connection, I feel almost anything can be asked.

A Call to Action!

My call to action for the readers in order to achieve an inclusive culture, is to have bold conversations. Once the conversation is started, stay in the conversation no matter how difficult it is. It's going to be uncomfortable, awkward, and tense. Stay in it, to work through it. Acknowledge with the other person that it's uncomfortable and explore the why and how of this together.

An interesting experiment to try as a man in a meeting, is when a female colleague says something and you notice this is ignored by the group. Then, a couple of minutes later, repeat exactly what the female colleague said and see what kind of reaction occurs. Most often, there will be a response. Call your colleagues out and highlight what happened: "Sarah just said this exact same thing a couple of minutes ago and was ignored by the group."

To me, this is an example of inclusive leadership. And you don't have to be in a leadership position to be an inclusive leader. We are all responsible to show up and behave in a way that respects, values, and includes people.

In the end, it is about working together, creating an environment where people feel safe, respected, and valued. A space that is a reflection of society, has equity in opportunities and has a sense of belonging.

Footnotes

[1] Colman A (2008). A Dictionary of Psychology (3 ed.). Oxford University Press. ISBN 9780199534067.

26 Archana Wuntakal

***Archana Wuntakal** is a champion of encouraging women in technology. She truly believes that 'We rise by lifting others' and invests a lot of her time in guiding and motivating young professionals.*

She started coding at the age of 16 and moved to Germany from India at the age of 21 to pursue her master's degree in Software Technology. She now lives in the Netherlands and has built a career in the field of technology. With more than 11 years of experience in IT and management, she helps companies with their technical strategy and embracing new technology. She specializes in stakeholder management and bridging the gap between business and technology. She uses her strong public speaking and facilitation skills as a tool to bridge cultural gaps within teams and to bring technology and people together.

When she is not having conversations about technology, she engages in traveling, public speaking, and stand-up comedy.

→ *To contact Archana: linkedin.com/in/archanawuntakal*

If Not You, Then Who?

If not you, then who? This is a question I have asked myself when faced with adversity. I have substituted 'Why me?' with 'If not you, then who?'. This substitution has also worked for me when I am presented with an opportunity and my brain goes 'you are just lucky', 'are you sure you can do this?' or 'people will someday find out you are not that smart'.

I believe that our life experiences and the background we grew up in, makes each of us truly unique. Like the saying by B.J. Neblett: "We are the sum total of our experiences." No one in this world can solve a problem or handle an opportunity like you do because no one else has experienced this world like you have. This belief has helped me build a fulfilling professional life in the field of technology, thousands of miles away from home.

My story

I grew up in Bangalore, India. When I was 11 years old, much against my wishes, I was pushed by my parents to go to Computer Camp during summer break. The only good part was we could play computer games at the end of every class. Although at that moment, I didn't realize what a privilege it was. The introduction to the world of computers cemented my interest in technology. This trend continued for the next couple of years during summer breaks. As I became familiar with basic concepts of computing, it became less abstract and more enjoyable. I particularly liked the concept of flowcharts and how they can be linked to decision-making. At the age of 16, I chose computer science as one of my electives. My education established the confidence that I could pursue a career in the field of computer science. Little did I know that this confidence would later be shattered and need to be rebuilt from scratch.

After finishing my bachelor's degree, I worked as a Software Test Engineer for a year. Then I decided to move to Stuttgart, Germany to do my master's in Software Technology. Having lived in the same city with my parents all my life, I knew moving out and setting up my life would be difficult. However, I didn't know it would affect my self-confidence too. At the age of 21, moving to a new country with a different culture, climate, and language was certainly an adventure for me.

On the first day of my master's course, I was shocked to realize there were only 2 women, one of whom was me, who had opted to study Software Technology in a class of around 20 students. This was quite opposite to what I had experienced back home. Where I grew up, topics related to computer science or engineering were not perceived as something for men only. I was used to studying and working with a lot of women in tech when I was in Bangalore. That master's class was also my introduction to the stereotypes which exist in the field of technology and how they affect women.

The first few months really took a toll on my self-confidence: navigating my way through the German culture, learning a new foreign language, lacking a strong social circle, and the burden of living off a student loan. I considered going back home. But I told myself that these challenges were only temporary. It would all be worth it when I could hold my master thesis in my hand. So, I persevered and finished my master's with flying colors.

10 years ago, after my master's, the prospect of working for a startup sounded cool. I took a job offer in the Netherlands and started working as a Software Engineer. The Netherlands is the place where I have failed the most, learned the most, and enjoyed the most.

Covering at work

Now I had a master's degree, which was proof enough that I am intellectually capable, as well as a job which provided a steady financial means to repay my student loan. I thought the time had finally come to enjoy my life abroad and focus on the next steps of my career. I had no idea that immersing myself in the Dutch culture, especially the directness, would set me back a few steps on my self-confidence journey.

In my new job, I was the only woman in a team of engineers and software architects. For a long time, I didn't realize how the lack of female role model or senior colleagues who I could relate to in my field of work, affected me. I wanted to fit in but after a few months, I started 'covering at work'[1]. I did not engage in any topics which would underline the fact that I am a woman from a different cultural background. I kept my conversations limited to work related topics and occasionally, I spoke about Indian food. This was not just in my first job as I continue to do this even today. I am more aware of this phenomenon now and make a conscious effort to not hide my identity. However, when I was still new to the Netherlands, this added to the emotional burden I was experiencing.

From time to time, I felt the pressure of wanting to fit in with my male colleagues. There were times when I have looked up Star Wars references/jokes or caught up on the latest news about tech gadgets. I did this so I could understand what my colleagues were talking about during lunch. I pretended that hackathons are more exciting than games at a friend's party (no, they are not!). With time, I have learned to embrace my own uniqueness and the unique value I bring to the (lunch) table.

In the field of tech, there are many stereotypical notions which need to be challenged: developers are socially awkward, they don't care about their appearance, they love hackathons, and so on. Some of these stereotypes often work against women and other minority groups. Please know, a developer can be sociable, have a good sense of fashion, and not enjoy hackathons, but only wants to deliver the best in their work.

The importance of mentorship early in your career:

Early in my career, I received feedback which was very direct and indicated I had to do much better. It was hard to hear. Until then, I was used to hearing positive feedback, both in my academic and professional life. Coding was something I had always enjoyed; it encouraged creative thinking in me. Over time, coding became less appealing.

This went on for more than 2 years, depriving me of my energy and interest in my work. Until one day, in one of the feedback discussions, I expressed my interest to learn more about the business. I wanted to contribute to one of the marketing campaigns, which needed a technical demonstration of an application I had built. To my surprise, I was presented with that opportunity almost immediately. I finished that assignment with a lot of zeal and positive feedback. I returned to my code delivery responsibilities, feeling more confident and energetic. When I look back, it was something so simple I needed to do in order to feel confident in my work. I just had to ask for the opportunities/assignments that interested me. My career had been in a rut. I was struggling with the Impostor Syndrome, never realizing it. I had been telling myself that maybe I'm not smart enough to be a software engineer. No one could help me because I didn't tell anyone what was going on with me. I wish I knew the importance of seeking a mentor back then. That would have made my early years in the Netherlands much easier.

I hope reading about experiences like mine will underline the importance of mentorship for those who are starting a career in tech. This way, we can prevent women from dropping out of the technology workforce early in their career.

Is coding difficult?

The simple answer is, you won't know until you try it. Coding is about thinking logically and having an aptitude for solving problems. The rest is just syntax and operational procedures. If you believe learning coding is complicated, low-code platforms might be an alternative.

"Low-code platforms employ visual, declarative techniques instead of traditional lines of programming. Both developers and non-developers can use these products, and they require less training to start. Common features include reusable components, drag-and-drop tools, and process modeling. Individuals or small teams can experiment, prototype, and deliver apps in days or weeks."[2] In order to catch up with the current rate of digital transformation, companies need to build quality apps quickly. Low-code platforms are a great resource for that.

The Low-code market is expected to increase to $21.2 billion in 2022, as more companies see the benefits of adopting the platform for their business needs[2]. Familiarizing yourself with one of the many low-code platforms could be a great way of taking your first steps towards a career in technology.

The ability to code has increased my confidence in comprehending the digital transformation challenges my clients face and guiding their technical strategy in the right direction. With this experience, I highly encourage young professionals to try and see if coding is for them. If you are already sure you want to learn coding, but you don't have formal education, then maybe places like Codam can be a good starting point.

Through my employer, I encountered Refugee Talent Hub[3]. I volunteered to teach basics of Python for the participants. While preparing for those lessons, I came across Coursera, edX, and CodeCademy. These are great resources where you can learn coding.

If you don't tell, they won't know

I enjoyed teaching coding more than delivering code under strict deadlines. The experience with Refugee Talent Hub made me realize that it was time for a change in my career direction. I wanted to take on the role of a technical advisor/coach. The next thing I did was inform my senior colleagues and manager about my aspiration. It took a few months and some discussions. Eventually, I was given an opportunity to perform such a role.

Dutch culture has taught me the importance of 'bespreekbaarheid'. I'm not sure if there is a correct translation for this in English. I guess it would roughly translate to 'speakability'. It is important to speak about your career aspirations with your colleagues, manager, or whoever you perceive as a stakeholder for your career progression. People make your career happen. So, until you speak up about your aspirations and ideas with the right people, it won't happen.

I hope my experiences and the tips I have shared, encourage you to consider a career in technology. If you ever feel lost with your career choices, as I did, look back at your own experiences. Realize the unique value you can bring to the field of technology, irrespective of whether you know coding or have a formal education.

If your brain is bombarding you with questions such as 'are you sure you can do this?', 'isn't it too difficult for you?' or 'are you smart enough for this?' remember to look into the mirror and ask yourself 'If not you, then who?'. Technology belongs to us all. Therefore, it is very important that people from different walks of life and with diverse sets of experiences contribute to it.

A Call to Action!

Seek mentoring at all stages of your career and speak up about your aspirations and ideas.

Footnotes

[1] https://ioadvisory.com/being-ourselves-vs-covering-at-work

[2] https://www.forrester.com/blogs/why-you-need-to-know-about-low-code-even-if-youre-not-responsible-for-software-delivery

[3] https://refugeetalenthub.com

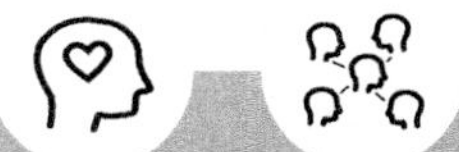

27

Mary Jane Roy

***Mary Jane Roy** is a highly motivated and dedicated corporate advisor, facilitator, and presenter, sharing with others how to develop more effective strategies to thrive in their lives. She started her career as a Registered Nurse and then as a Military Nursing Officer in the Canadian Armed Forces, with a specialty in cardiac diagnostics. After leaving her military nursing career, she worked for the next three plus decades in multiple industries. Since 2009, Mary Jane has accrued various certifications, all adding to her mastery of the skills needed to thrive. She loves to present on these topics for groups.*

Her belief? With the proper knowledge and tools, we can ALL improve our resiliency to what life brings onto our path AND thrive in life. Values and strengths which represent who she is include: dependable; perseverance; honest; resilient (of course!); humor; love of learning; curiosity; equality; gratitude.

To contact Mary Jane: linkedin.com/in/maryjaneroy
→ *creatingwaves.nl*

For the Sake of Transparency

For the sake of transparency, at the time of this writing, I am 66+ year's old. Since the age of 19, I've worked independently for much, but not all, of my career: either alone, with a colleague, or with my husband. There have been a lot of career moves. Starting from: a military nursing career in the Canadian Armed Forces as a Lieutenant; sales rep in the pharmaceutical industry; consultant in the fitness branch; then consultant in an engineering firm (you'll read more about this later). I then went back to the fitness branch, ending with the career I love now: supporting employees and organizations to become resilient and to thrive.

You can pack a lot in, in a 45+ year career. Or not. The choice is yours to do so. Or not.

Thanks to a cardiologist!

Some heart health problems at the age of 28 pointed me in the direction of a fitness club. Or rather, a Cardiologist did: "tell this woman to get herself into a fitness program." This, to someone who took tap, jazz, ballet, and swimming lessons each week! But it wasn't enough, apparently, to get me into cardiovascular shape. I met my future husband, who was co-owner of the fitness club I joined, as a result of that Cardiologist's encouragement. René is Dutch and had immigrated to Canada when he was 14. We actually met while I was living on Holland Ave, in Ottawa, Ontario. Little did I know then that I would be moving to the country a number of years later; Holland that is. Officially known as the Netherlands. Where I've now lived since 1993.

A pivotal moment

After dating for almost 2 years, René asked me to marry him. I remember the day distinctly. Actually, it was an evening early in 1985. We were sitting in the living room of the rustic log cabin we rented in the Gatineau's, in Quebec. A fire burned in the huge, stone fireplace. Next to each other on the couch, he posed the BIG question. I looked at him and said: "René, I'm going to grab onto your coattails and go for the ride." What I knew was that marrying him wasn't going to be the 'huisje, boompje, beestje' lifestyle (a Dutch expression which I invite you to look up – Google translation will help), which so many of my friends and family were enjoying or had settled for. I was going on an adventure.

I had left my military nursing career and had worked for two different pharmaceutical companies by the time I met René. He convinced me to come and work with him in the fitness chain he was a partner in. Though he had to work at persuading me, I finally acquiesced.

An important life lesson

Through a series of decisions and situations, in 1989 we ended up working as consultants for a heat reclamation engineering company based in Florida. For me, to describe what this entails would involve another essay. Suffice it to say, it was highly technical work. For someone who had barely passed her high school physics class, it was a challenge. But I persevered and learned one of my most important life lessons: I could learn anything I wanted to, as long as I wanted to.

We had the entire west coast of Canada and the US as our territory, working as sales consultants. Since California was the largest market, we made our home base in Cambria. It's a lovely, small town on the coast, in between San Francisco and LA.

Our clients were large, industrial factories using copious amounts of hot water. Think of blue jean factories, industrial laundries, and meat processing plants. Our initial contacts in these factories were always the boiler maintenance men. They provided us with the information the company engineers needed to propose a system. It was only men in this role, at the time. Back then, I didn't meet one woman in the function. And it became my first remembered exposure to gender bias.

You see, I had taken my responsibility towards the company which had hired us very seriously. I knew the questions I had to ask and why the information was important. Even one small mistake could have catastrophic financial consequences. I could calculate the ROI on the potential equipment purchase close to the dollar. But I couldn't convince these men to listen and take me seriously. 'Little lady' were words I came to hate. Indulgent smiles when I walked into the boiler rooms were signs that I was an anomaly. In the two years we worked for this company, I sold nada, nothing! While René, my husband, strolled into these manufacturing or production facilities, a pencil behind his ear, as if to say, 'I know what I'm doing'. And he sold millions of dollars of equipment. This, while having to come to me to work out the formulas and ROI's needed to convince the owners to purchase.

At the time, it didn't occur to me that this was gender bias in action. I just accepted it, as frustrating as it was, as part of being in a 'man's world'. Because we were independent consultants, it wasn't until years later, when I joined PWN Netherlands in 2009, that I began to understand how pervasive gender bias is.

A new realization

In 2006 my mother suffered a stroke which left her incapacitated on her left side. I spent the next 9 months travelling back and forth to Canada every 5 weeks to help care for her, together with my brother and sisters. It was a time of sleep deprivation and of putting myself last.

In the fall of 2007, in my early 50's, a series of health challenges finally took their toll. And another of life's big lessons hit me squarely. In all the years of following my husband on our adventures, I realized I'd left myself behind. I literally had hung onto his coattails but the ride I went on was his, not mine. In circa 25 years, I had never once stopped and asked myself, 'is what we're doing, what I want to do?'.

This realization took me on a journey, one I'm still on, of self-discovery. Who was I? What did I want to do? Who did I want to be? What legacy would I leave behind me?

The next couple of years were spent recovering my health and taking a deep dive into what stress is, what it does to us physiologically and how we can develop better strategies to handle it. Never did I think I would make a career of sharing this knowledge with others but I finally found what makes my heart sing. Supporting employees to develop resiliency skills and to thrive, is the main purpose that drives me.

Making a difference

Another purpose came about in 2009, as a result of joining a network supporting women in their career development. I had lived and worked in a Dutch 'bubble' for the first 16 years, with only one English speaking friend. My main goal in joining the PWN network was to connect with other English speaking women. This network is very international, counting more than sixty nationalities amongst its members. It was through this diverse group of women, that I began to understand the roadblocks many faced in advancing their careers. It also opened my eyes to the number of times I had been on the receiving end of gender biases.

The desire to make a difference, to support women in developing their careers and ensuring more women are in leadership roles, grew with each year. In 2014, I was asked to take a board position, heading up the Learning & Development program for the members and participating guests. In 2017, I stepped into the role of Vice-President, with a wide variety of responsibilities. As I write this essay, though I no longer serve on the board, I am still a committed member.

Meeting and connecting with these wonderful women and men (since 2020, men can be members of our network) has been a high point in my life. A female child psychologist once told me that the glass ceiling many women face, is not the one imposed upon us but one we impose upon ourselves: a lack of self-efficacy or a lack of belief in one's abilities. And maybe it's not fair to say we impose it upon ourselves, since much of this is as a result of the nurturing we received. As a child psychologist, she has seen the role nurturing plays in developing self-efficacy or not. Whatever the reason for it, the support I receive and give in this network has definitely increased my confidence.

A new me

Having taken a back seat on my coattail ride, I sorely lacked in confidence or a belief in myself. Developing my resiliency muscle was an important step forward, in my stride to creating a new me. Someone who dared to take risks on her own. Someone who dared to step into the light.

Over the ensuing years, I can't tell you in how many ways I've changed. The post-cancer Mary Jane, who had to dig deep in herself to rise above her mental, emotional, and physical challenges? She is a person I like much more than the pre-cancer Mary Jane.

A Call to Action!

What is my call to action for you, the reader? Be true to yourself! If you want to become a female leader of the future (which is now), stop and ask yourself this question, on a regular basis: 'what do I need now?'. Live life on your own terms, not those of someone else. It's not that I'm asking you to disregard others but ensure that you continually invest in the number one person in your life, and that is you. If you don't love yourself enough to take care of yourself, then how can you be there for anyone else you love?

28

Anna Tropsch

__Anna Tropsch__ is an experienced, internationally certified coach who coaches C suite level executives of Fortune 500 companies.

From traveling all over the world, living in 6 capitals, speaking 6 languages, and changing 4 professions, she became a true open minded cosmopolitan. Anna started from scratch multiple times, rebuilding her life in new countries, in new environments with different mentalities and languages. Every time, she built her career to the executive level, becoming and being a genuine leader.

Anna has been published in several journals such as Office Life, Probusiness and giving numerous interviews about Women in Leadership, what it takes to be a female leader and how to get there, what makes female leadership different, as well as why is it beneficial for the companies to have more woman on the board.

Realizing her need, to help other women, to achieve their career success, Anna decided to join PWN as mentor, coach, and facilitator as well as to share her valuable experience and ideas in this book.

→ *To contact Anna: linkedin.com/in/anna-tropsch/*

Women in Leadershift

My dear reader, if you, like me, are a woman who has chosen to build a career and ascended to the top of corporate Olympus, you are among the fortunate few, and here is why. When we go deeper into the Women in Leadership topic to see how many of us have made it this far, we discover just 29% worldwide, while 47% of women, according to Catalyst, keep working as support stuff.[1]

It also matters where you work, since working in Norway, France, or Sweden, the top three EU leaders for female board seats, increases your chances to 36%.[2] It's no surprise that Norway was the first country to pass laws requiring women to be represented on corporate boards of stock exchange companies. By the way, how far do you think this initiative has gone throughout the globe? Now this is the kicker: according to Fortune Globalist, just 13 women, or 2.6 %, were CEOs of Fortune Global 500 companies as of August 2020.[3]

If you still believe your country, city, company, or environment is preventing you from advancing your career, remember, you are part of the three percent and consider relocating. It's obvious all worldwide economies have a long way to go before achieving gender parity on corporate boards, but why is that?

Perhaps it's because males outnumber women in the workforce because women are more inclined to stay at home and care for their families? The data shows that in some regions, such as India and the UAE, the influence of traditions and culture is significantly contributing to the gender gap in the labor force. Despite this fact, in most of the countries, women contribute more than 40% of the labor force but do not reach the top. What's the deal?

Before we find out the answer to this question, it is worth mentioning that the COVID-19 pandemic has also affected women's labor-force participation. Women are 24% more likely than men to lose their jobs, according to Catalyst.[4]

So why so slow, why so few, and what does bias have to do? Well, this depends on who you ask. According to a survey of over 4000 directors conducted by Women Corporate Directors Foundation, if your boss is a male over the age of 55, his answer will most likely be the lack of qualified female candidates is the main reason of female directors' stagnant number. Female and younger male directors, on the other hand, blamed women's slow career development on male-dominated networking, which frequently led to male director appointments.[5]

Those are only views, but what is the truth?

Women outnumber men at universities across the world; in 39 of the 47 UNECE nations, women account for more than 55 percent of higher education graduates. Iceland has the highest share, at 66 %.[6] So we're dealing here with a 'she is under qualified' bias phenomenon, which along with the 'it's a man's world' network makes it harder for women:

a. To be nominated for promotion, especially the very first promotion (the Sticky Floor Effect).
b. To get promoted (because most of the deciders are men age 55+).

This is a critical discovery for the understanding of the next phenomena known as the 'Glass Ceiling'. The term, introduced in 1986 in the Wall Street Journal, was defined as the social barrier preventing women from being promoted to a top management job, regardless of their qualifications or achievements. A classic example of Glass Ceiling effects is the gender salary gap between men and women with the same level of seniority, experience, and qualifications. Women are globally almost 20% underpaid. The employers are explaining this as risk management intent, in case a woman in a leadership position would take maternal leave. Strange enough, this applies to women of age 45+ as well.[7]

Also, women tend to self-restrict themselves on their career path. This is due to their own or social biases, trying, for example, to fit the expectations of parents or society. This phenomenon is called the 'Crystal Shoe'. The association is well illustrated in Grimm's Cinderella story, when her sisters try everything they can to fit into the crystal shoe, including cutting off a toe or heel, in order to be promoted to Princess.

To better understand the next one, called 'Blue for Boy, Pink for Girl', consider how the industry sector can become a limiting factor for women's career success. According to Catalyst, only 29.3 percent of women choose to pursue degrees in STEM (Science, Technology, Engineering, and Mathematics). As a result, only 16 percent of CIOs are female, while 40% of HR Directors are female. The reason is simple: STEM professions are typically seen as 'blue-collar' men, whereas HR professions are typically 'pink-collar' women. Women self-restrict themselves from successful future careers by allowing themselves to be guided by old social rules and expectations.

Surprisingly, the few men who choose a 'pink-collar' career, such as school teaching, typically benefit from the 'Glass Escalator' effect; getting promoted to senior positions simply for being heterosexual white males.[8] If any of this sounds familiar to you, keep in mind that while you cannot change the biases of others, you can change your own limiting beliefs, and a coach or mentor can be of great assistance.

What holds women back on their career path?

We can divide the barriers preventing women from advancing in their careers into three categories:

Organizational:
- Unfriendly corporate culture and underpayment
- Male preference in personnel decisions
- Higher requirements and standards of performance for women
- Silent majority of male peers and male CEOs
- Lack of systematic career development opportunities for women

Interpersonal:
- Biases and stereotypes
- Exclusion from informal networks 'men's clubs'
- Lack of mentoring

Personal:
- Lack of self-confidence
- Lack of political savvy
- Lack of negotiation skills
- Difficulties balancing work and family life

Why do companies need female leaders?

We all know that formal education is important, but being an outstanding leader requires so much more! What about women's other leadership competencies? Can women be outstanding leaders? When Businessweek conducted a meta-analysis of many women's leadership competencies, they discovered that women outperformed men on a 360-degree basis in almost every study, including:[9]

- motivating and inspiring others
- open communication and feedback
- listening and including others
- working hard and producing high-quality results

According to the same studies, women outperform their male counterparts in traditionally male competencies such as:
- Data analysis
- Strategic planning

Another study, conducted by Zenger Folkman, a consulting firm, looked at a survey of more than 7,000 women and men leaders from public, private, governmental, and commercial companies around the world. They discovered indisputable evidence that women are strong in leadership competencies. It was also discovered that a person's level within the organization plays an important role. Men and women had equal competencies at the middle and lower levels.[10] Women's competencies were higher than men's at higher levels. And yet, women have a difficult time rising to the top; perhaps there is a lack of demand, and companies simply do not require female leaders? To respond to this question, Catalyst gathered data from organizations that chose to have more women in senior positions and corporate culture, and as a result, they:

1. Outperform financially organizations with fewer women on board.
2. Have higher quality corporate social responsibility and initiatives.
3. Are more likely to engage more women in corporate leadership positions within the next five years

Having more women on board is not only profitable for some organizations but also beneficial for the entire society. Now let's see if women's leadership style is any different to men's and how it may affect the corporate culture.

Over 160 different studies discovered only one major difference in the leadership styles of men and women: women used a more participative, inclusive, or democratic style and men used a less autocratic or directive style. Interesting is also that this tendency decreased in a heavily male-dominated environment, where both men and women use the same autocratic and directive leadership styles. Those studies also determined that if the overage board of directors includes 10-15 people, at least 3-5 of them should be women in order to have enough influence on the company's leadership style, making it more inclusive and democratic.

What strategies do successful female leaders use?

The Harvard Business Review published an interesting study conducted by Ruderman and Ohlott, pointing out which five competencies most contribute to the career success of women leaders:[11]

1] Authenticity is the link between daily behaviors and deeply held values and beliefs, as well as a good understanding of their priorities and emotions. It assists women in overcoming obstacles such as imposter syndrome, humility in assessing their intelligence, lack of self-confidence, and insecure body language.
2] Connection with colleagues, coworkers, teams, sponsors, mentors due to open communication and feedback, which helps to achieve collective goals and create a powerful network. Quality connections allow women to increase self-confidence and the likelihood to take part in a competition. As the Hewlett-Packard study found, men will apply for a job when they consider themselves 60% qualified for it, while women only when they feel 100% qualified!
3] Accountability is the willingness to take responsibility and control their own life and actions and willingness to decide and take reasonable risks. It helps women to be resilient towards the stress of failure and persistent in taking action and reaching results.
4] Integrity is the sense of feeling to be complete. Integrating various life roles is the driving force of many high-achieving women. The important part of it is also the ability to keep life-work balance, being self-efficient.
5] Self-awareness and understanding of organizational culture: knowing who you are, what are your strengths and weaknesses. It's an important base for further development of adaptability and understanding of oneself in the organization's context and its culture helps to design a clear career path.

What can every woman do to become part of Leadershift?

1] Raise awareness and spread awareness about the current situation of women in leadership.
2] Hire, recommend, coach, mentor, support, promote other women.
3] Choose your education, profession, and hobbies based on your talents and passion, rather than being influenced by 'pink-collar' stereotypes, parents, or social preferences.

4] Educate your children, aligned with gender equality principles.
5] Be yourself, be authentic, know your values, live and lead by them.
6] Connect with others, nourish your network, participate in networking events, and follow-up.
7] Learn to listen with empathy and without judgment.
8] Learn to communicate clearly and assertively.
9] Be open and friendly; remember that anyone can become your ally.
10] Don't forget to negotiate.

A Call to Action!

Remember: You are unique, and you are the sole author of your life and career; it is all in your hands; believe in yourself, and make the best of it!

Footnotes

[1] Women in management (quick take). Catalyst. (2021, July 23). Retrieved October 19, 2021, from https://www.catalyst.org/research/women-in-management/

[2] Women on Corporate Boards (Quick Take). Catalyst. (2021, August 19). Retrieved October 19, 2021, from https://www.catalyst.org/research/women-on-corporate-boards/

[3] Women in the workforce: Global (Quick Take). Catalyst. (2021, June 15). Retrieved October 19, 2021, from https://www.catalyst.org/research/women-in-the-workforce-global/

[4] Women in the workforce: Global (Quick Take). Catalyst. (2021, June 15). Retrieved October 19, 2021, from https://www.catalyst.org/research/women-in-the-workforce-global/

[5] Spencer Stuart Board index. (n.d.). Retrieved October 19, 2021, from https://www.spencerstuart.com/~/media/PDF%20Files/Research%20and%20Insight%20PDFs/SSBI2014web14Nov2014.pdf. Staff, M. D. (2019, September 9)

[6] Women outnumber men in higher education but gender stereotyped subject choices persist. Modern Diplomacy. Retrieved October 19, 2021, from https://moderndiplomacy.eu/2019/09/10/women-outnumber-men-in-higher-education-but-gender-stereotyped-subject-choices-persist/. Gould, R. • B. E. (n.d.)

[7] What is the gender pay gap and is it real?: The Complete Guide to how women are paid less than men and why it can't be explained away. Economic Policy Institute. Retrieved October 19, 2021, from https://www.epi.org/publication/what-is-the-gender-pay-gap-and-is-it-real/

[8] Women in science, technology, engineering, and mathematics (STEM) (quick take). Catalyst. (2021, July 23). Retrieved October 19, 2021, from https://www.catalyst.org/research/women-in-science-technology-engineering-and-mathematics-stem/

[9] (PDF) buried treasure: Contradictions in the perception ... (n.d.). Retrieved October 19, 2021, from https://www.researchgate.net/publication/351875355_Buried_Treasure_Contradictions_in_the_Perception_and_Reality_of_Women's_Leadership

[10] Solved: Previous surveys reported that more men than women... | chegg.com. (n.d.). Retrieved October 19, 2021, from https://www.chegg.com/homework-help/questions-and-answers/previous-surveys-reported-men-women-trade-stocks-online-local-brokerage-firm-randomly-sele-q29170109

[11] (PDF) Women's Leadership Development Strategic Practices for women and organizations ResearchGate. (n.d.). Retrieved October 19, 2021, from https://www.researchgate.net/publication/232509932_Women's_leadership_development_strategic_practices_for_women_and_organizations

Acknowledgements

Pema and I would like to express our heartfelt thanks to the book's amazing project team of contributors, who made the publishing of this anthology possible: Tessa van Keeken, Shokoofeh Ketabchi, Margarita Lourido, Francia Agterhof, Dick Rüger, Rosemary Amato, Archana Wuntakal, and Wendy Broersen, we thank you for your enthusiasm and dedication to achieve what we now hold in our hands.

We also owe a debt of gratitude to a number of advisors, who lent a helping hand throughout the process. Advisors among the contributors: Béatrice Blondiau, Bernice Feller-Thijm, Charlotte Heilmann, Nico Samaras, and Vivian Acquah. External advisors: Theresa Sigillito Hollema, Alison Gallardi, Lynn Kaplanian-Buller, Nicoline Huizinga, Antonie Knopper, Thaís Souzas, Marijke Dijt, Denise Hulst, and Alex Slavenburg.

Printed in Great Britain
by Amazon

75768479R00139